ALSO BY JILL JOHNSTON

Marmalade Me

Lesbian Nation

Gullibles Travels

Mother Bound

Autobiography in Search of a Father

MOTHER BOUND

Jill Johnston

ALFRED A. KNOPF   New York   1983

THIS IS A BORZOI BOOK
PUBLISHED BY ALFRED A. KNOPF, INC.

Library of Congress Cataloging in Publication Data

Johnston, Jill.   Mother bound.

1. Johnston, Jill—Biography.
2. Authors, American—20th century—Biography.
I. Title.
PS3560.03894Z47   1983   818'.5409   82-48592
ISBN 0-394-52757-7

Manufactured in the United States of America

FIRST EDITION

PHOTO CREDITS

Rainer and Johnston improvising: © 1964 by Peter Moore. Rivers,
Rauschenberg, Segal: Hans Persson. Cage: Roberto Masotti.
Cunningham: Lufti Ozkok. Ginsberg: © 1964 by Fred W. McDarrah.
Johnston "daring leap": Ralph Crane. Geldzahler, Grooms, Johnston:
© 1963 by Peter Moore. Rainer and friends: Wadsworth Atheneum.
Johnston "sixties look": © 1969 by Fred W. McDarrah. All pictures
not otherwise credited are from the author's private collection.

If men create families and lineages in order to ensure that their names and property are passed along to their descendants, is it not logical for women to use their nameless, propertyless line of descent to perpetuate scandal, to pass along what is unacceptable.

The Three Marias

And have no fellowship with the unfruitful works of darkness, but rather reprove them. For it is a shame even to speak of those things which are done of them in secret. But all things that are reproved are made manifest by the light: for whatsoever doth make manifest is light.

Ephesians 5:11-13

Acknowledgments

I would like to thank the following people for their assistance and encouragement in bringing this work to fruition: Robert Cornfield, Robert Gottlieb, Martha Kaplan, Danny Moses, George Walsh, Stanley Weinstock, and in particular Ingrid Nyeboe, whose persistence and trust made the last laps possible.

Mother Bound

1

A Late
American Invader

In the last two years of her life my mother frequently asked me if I was writing a book about our family. Wishing not to offend her I always hedged my answers, but I think she knew I was. I always thought she secretly wanted me to, and in fact that our story was her legacy to me. Once she said she hoped I would wait until she was dead before publishing such a book. She tried to discourage me by observing that our family couldn't possibly be of interest to anyone. It was an ordinary middle-class family in which no one had become prominent or public. She was an avid reader of biographies of important people, especially royal and aristocratic people, whose circumstances were remote from hers. Her own family in some ways embarrassed her, and her own life in particular had given her pause. This was of great interest to me. My mother had nothing to be ashamed of—she was a good-looking, vigorous woman, honest, hard working and self-sufficient all her life; but she had done one thing when she was young that she regretted. As if to make up for her uninteresting family, she had gone out of her way to do something different enough to warrant spending the rest of her life covering it up. (She had plenty of nerve, which she later defined as foolhardiness.) When she was twenty-five, she met a dashing gentleman who fancied her enough to have a serious affair with her, but whom she was unable to marry. She was a virgin when she met him, and when the affair was over she would be an unwed mother.

Surely something in my mother's family must have been interesting, to account for her daring and originality. Not only did she have an unusual adventure, but in a sense she contrived to make it last a lifetime, by creating a pseudo-identity to help her survive her "mistake." With this identity she insulated herself from the world, protecting her fantasy, preserving her pride, and nurturing her regrets. Put differently, the adventure she prolonged was through me. Without me, the identity she created and so fiercely protected would have been possible, perhaps, but not essential. Yet equally essential to her scheme was that I be kept in the dark about it. Her secret was not safe if not kept successfully from me. In a way then I became the unwitting keeper of her secret—of the identity she arranged to help her survive my birth. So long as my mother kept me close to her, her scheme was safe, and she could enjoy me tremendously, her secret pride and joy. But as I grew older and circumstances drove us apart, I sagged under the responsibility of her investment, of which I knew nothing, and at long last, as I shall relate, I blew her cover. With her cover story my mother perjured herself beyond recall, conveying just enough to leave me with an exciting residue. She was always perfectly clear, for example, about the fact that she had brought me here from a foreign country. Essentially she told me two things:

I was born in England, and I had a dead English father. The record on both scores was not unconvincing, especially as to my birth. In a "baby book" of photos that she had lovingly assembled, the event was nicely recorded on the first page with white ink inscriptions under three snapshots of myself in the arms of a British nurse who was seated on the grounds of the nursing home in Finchley, a suburb of London, to which my mother had retreated for the occasion. An itinerary in Britain and on the continent was amply preserved, as

well as our passage home to America. The absence of any
gentleman who might conceivably pass for a father was also
impressive—it was certainly not an absence I ever questioned.
Nor did I consider the different ways a person might be absent.
This particular absence had been effectively dispatched by my
mother as death; the important thing for both of us was that
a psychological death had taken place. England was behind
us, and nothing (more) was supposed to be said or thought
about it. Eventually two more things *were* said about it, and
these were the clues my mother dropped, inadvertently to be
sure, that led me back to the forbidden fatherland. She was
very proud of my father and she let me know what he did
and how important he was. Her pride naturally was commen-
surate with her disappointment, but her disappointment was
not a proper subject, for me at least, and it was inconsistent
with her story. Therefore I heard only the good part. The
other "clue" was the bad part, and that was my father's sister,
who was "a crazy person," according to my mother. This was
the role my mother assigned to me when she was piqued by
something I did that seemed foolish or irresponsible. She
would say I was like this woman, my father's sister. (She never
said I was like my father.) I was certainly a good deal like
her; this was confirmed by my mother's mother who frequently observed that we were "two of a kind." Anyway I
was raised in America exclusively under the influence of my
mother's maternal family, that very uninteresting family
which had provided my mother a background for her curious
adventure abroad.

My mother was an American whose own mother's parents
had emigrated from Europe in 1850—one from Sweden, one
from Germany—and whose father was an American of English
descent. It was, I believe, my mother's embarrassment over
her Swedish and German ancestry that ultimately drove her to
go out on a big English limb. Her mother was a fine robust
woman, but she was uneducated and without any sophistica-

tion. It was not necessarily her mother's humble origins that disturbed my mother, but her failure to better herself or show some class on her own. Actually, her mother did well enough for herself—she bought her own house and lived to an old age, for example—but whatever she did, it wasn't good enough for my mother. The main thing that wasn't good enough was her mother's English, which she spoke without an accent but with colloquialisms like "ain't" that drove my mother wild.

My grandmother was born in New York City in 1872, the last of five children born to Minna and Frank Seibold, who was a baker from Germany. When she was eight or so, Minna and Frank died, and my grandmother was farmed out to older sisters. I lose her there until she turned twenty-eight and found my mother's father in a boardinghouse in Manhattan. As she was not educated or religious, marriage must have seemed imperative, but it must also have been a difficult choice for her to make since she was twenty-eight before she got around to it. Her ethos in any case was to wait for "the right one," and while her marriage was not successful, I think she never doubted her choice. Her marriage was the one thing that my mother might have approved of, had she not taken it for granted or discounted it (as she discounted anything related to her mother). I never heard my mother praise my grandmother for marrying my grandfather, yet that marriage was perhaps the most ambitious move made by a Seibold in America. My mother always said her father, Frederick Crowe, came from a "good family"—which meant that his father, Chauncey Crowe, had been a schoolteacher from England. From any other point of view, the Crowe family didn't seem very good: Chauncey killed himself after his wife died, leaving his son and a daughter orphaned before they were ten. My grandmother was attracted to a man with a background as insecure as hers, or worse, considering he was adopted by strangers and turned out to be a weak survivor. He and my grandmother were married in 1900, and he lived only until 1920 when he was forty-six. In my mother's background the men were not survivors and the women were strong but embarrassing. The picture is completed by her emotional preference for the ones who failed to survive.

The actual portrait of this couple is a familiar one: my mother's mother hardy and vigorous looking, medium build and well bosomed, a full head of chestnut-auburn hair swept up in the Victorian style, a glint of good humor in her eye; my mother's father tall, lean and arid looking, clean-cut and handsome but not striking or especially spirited, his straight sandy brown hair parted down the middle, his bearing straight upright and correct. He was a man with little affect, while my grandmother was emotional and expressive. My mother resembled her father physically, and she wanted to be like him too, but she shared her mother's exuberance and merriment—she was a lot more like her mother than she wished to be or thought she was. She was an only child who was half like her mother and half like her father, but who took sides with her father; she had to take sides because her mother and father had an ongoing argument with each other. Frederick Crowe never found a career or steady employment, and his wife, my grandmother Pauline, who had grown up in a poor family, was anxious about their circumstances. She nagged and bitched and worried and complained. Frederick was proud and diffident. He was superior enough, but the world had failed to appreciate him, and he went from job to job doing things that were beneath him. One thing that was absolutely beneath him was his wife.

If his wife was as worried as my mother said she was, she was given good cause to go on worrying. Without affording her husband any confidence, he might easily have concluded she was not worth what it could mean to them if he succeeded at something. Possibly Frederick was a failure even before she began worrying about him—I can imagine that she was worried and he was failing long before they met each other.

He wasn't a businessman or a tradesman by nature, and he hadn't the formal education needed to be a teacher like his father. The only thing he really enjoyed, according to my mother, was mathematics. "My, how he used to sit over his problems," she told me. He liked numbers the way my mother liked words and pictures. My mother imitated her own mother in this respect—they were both idiots at numbers. But her mother was also unread, and untutored in general, and while her father was not a reliable provider or a happy person, he had superior interests—a man who could "pass," as my mother always put it. More important, perhaps, he was fond of his daughter, though he left her socialization to his wife. And in the Victorian Protestant style, his wife socialized their daughter—my mother—by reproof rather than encouragement. She took her job seriously, too, so seriously that the bond of love between her and her daughter was as uncultivated as her English, leaving her daughter more vexed with her than affectionate. Not until my grandmother was dying did my mother express her true affection for her, and even later, long after she died, her admiration. By sharing her father's disdain for her mother (he told my mother that he and his wife were incompatible because she was ignorant), and valuing her father's qualities over his abilities, which in any case she was too young to judge or appreciate, and further, by idealizing him in the void left by his early death, she approached womanhood with unreal expectations of men. No man could be as good as her father, who at the same time had disappointed her grievously by dying. It was her emotional preference for the sex who failed to survive that drove her eventually to her great adventure abroad.

My mother was born Olive Marjorie Crowe in 1901, a year also noted for the death of Victoria. She was born in Elizabeth, New Jersey, and raised in Huntington, Long Island, two sites chosen by my grandmother's older sisters in their quest for better lives out of New York. The sister my grandmother was closest to was probably my great-aunt Mary, whose son

Eddie played a certain paternal role in my life when I was small and was living with my grandmother. I never knew her other sisters, or her brothers. The sister my mother was closest to was her aunt Molly, who lived with her husband, Uncle Henry, in Elizabeth, where my mother was born. Molly's son Harry was my mother's favorite cousin and best childhood friend. Harry was an only child too, and when he was a young man he killed himself. I heard a lot about Harry when I was growing up—he had married a woman called Gladys by whom he had a daughter. I always had the idea he should have married my mother instead of a stranger who might have made him unhappy. (I don't know whether his wife made him unhappy or not, but neither do I know why he killed himself.) In an "uninteresting" family this was perhaps the most interesting thing that had ever happened. Harry hanged himself in the attic of his house, a vivid and morbid image to ponder. My mother was so upset about it that she failed to be discreet in my presence. Years later she told me that Harry went to see her before he hanged himself and that he was clearly disturbed, but she was unable to draw him out. That doesn't mean she tried to, only that she was unable to because emotional problems were a taboo subject. People then, as now, but much more so then, could become seriously isolated with their disturbances. In fact, isolation itself was the chief disturbance, a condition of people whose anxiety over appearances and struggles to survive tended to drive them apart rather than together. My mother's parents isolated each other emotionally, but her mother was expressive and she had relatives around her. Her father withdrew and walled himself up inside the private world into which he felt driven. There he pored over his mathematical problems and eventually succumbed to tuberculosis. Harry evidently was a silent sufferer like my mother's father. My mother had this tendency strongly herself, and after her father died she suffered her first serious depression.

My mother had rugged athletic interests and she was adventurous, but she wasn't as durable or sturdy as her own mother. Life in Huntington in the early 1900s was a rural sandbox. Horse-and-buggies and fields and dirt roads, a general store, a few houses and a one-room schoolhouse. . . . A girl like my mother would grow up leading two kinds of lives: a tomboy outside and a studious girl, prim and proper, at home. She was the star of her family, and she was popular with her peers. Tall and lanky and not conventionally pretty or beautiful, she was strikingly attractive, if that distinction can be made. She looked like someone who might have gone on to do great things—become an Earhart or a Didrikson or a Mead or an Osa Johnson, a woman who wrote a book about hunting big game in Africa called *I Married Adventure* that I read in boarding school. In a way, my mother did become a big-game hunter when she went abroad and found my father, and she certainly married adventure if nothing else.

It was ironic that such an outgoing girl, whose one great adventure was the stuff of tall tales, should spend her life so quietly—ironic, yet consistent with her background. Her naiveté and enthusiasm eventually outstripped her circumstances, qualities naturally untested in the country setting where they had been cultivated. Her mother was not worldly at all and her father knew more than he was able to communicate. As attractive and appealing as she was, once she left her family environment and went abroad, an encounter that far surpassed her limitations seemed inevitable. But no less prophetic of the future than her innocence and expectant nature was her capacity for disappointment resulting from her father's untimely death. In the transition between his death and her entry into the world, she had one serious mishap and two serious illnesses. These events spanned the period of his dying, before and during and after. She was eighteen when he died and twenty when she left home.

If a depression is a kind of mourning, then my mother mourned her father in this manner. Her mother was more fortunate. One memory of my mother's serves to illustrate a difference between them that was costly to my mother. She remembered her mother upstairs in her bedroom crying after her father died. To my mother, crying was an indefensible expression of weakness—she remembered the incident fifty-five years later with immediate scorn. Yet at the time, perhaps, what she had felt was more terror than scorn. Her father was dead and her mother was falling apart, and she was alone with her mother. My mother had to be strong—that is, unfeeling—if they were to survive; if anything bothered her she had to keep it to herself the way her father always had. In time she would be a silent sufferer like him and like her cousin Harry. In fact, within a year—or two at most—she was staying at her aunt Molly's house in New Jersey, paralyzed with depression. She told me that she spent weeks (possibly months) there in that state, staring at the walls. But neither Harry nor her father ever claimed depression as an illness. If they were depressed it was a mood, albeit a serious one, underlying everything they did—pervasive, debilitating, corrosive, and fatal, but never serious enough to immobilize them. Possibly Harry's suicide was preceded by a clinical depression, and as for Frederick, he was surely immobilized at the end by his respiratory illness. But for them both, a chronic clinical depression would have seemed an impossible luxury, whereas for my mother it became an essential vacation, a way to commune with her feelings without admitting to them. This way, too, she could partake as much of her mother's nature as her father's. She was already too spirited to be depressed the way her father had been. Her father's death polarized her temperament between her mother's and his. What made her mother merry made her manic and eager. What made her father withdrawn and discouraged made her immobile. Not that she couldn't sometimes be merry or withdrawn and discouraged the way they were, but that she moved toward the extremes of their dispositions and created scenarios in which those extremes could be experienced. Of the two extremes I knew or recognized only their everyday aspects, the more precise imitations of her mother and father. She loved to tease and play and laugh over a joke—she shared with her mother an uproarious sense of humor. She also fussed and nagged and complained the way her mother did. She was irritable and impatient sometimes too, and I assume that in this she was more like her father, because I don't remember my grandmother that way, though she may have mellowed by the time I knew her. I also remember my mother on occasion sad and withdrawn, unreachable and far away inside herself. I think that was how she looked when she was depressed. The depression itself was a total collapse of faith or confidence; in order to reexperience faith, she would have to prize something as dearly as she had her father. The way to retrieve him was to await him as a bride might, and then the only way to have him would be to lose the impostor she had chosen to supplant him. Anyway, my mother's departure from home was complete with two other personal disasters that were significant for the future.

One was a concussion and the other an improperly treated case of hepatitis, which turned into jaundice and damaged her liver; when she was an old lady it was her liver that killed her. Her concussion may have given her a new idea or two that altered her life direction. She was nineteen and driving a Model T Ford one day when a young man piled up his motorcycle onto her running board, ramming his handlebars into her head. This young man, by chance, was the son of the fabulously wealthy Otto Kahn, who compensated my mother handsomely for the accident. Besides paying her bills, including a convalescence at a lake resort someplace, he gave her ten thousand dollars, a huge sum in those days. The appearance of a "very rich father," a kind of patron, just when her own father was dying and about to leave her and her mother very poor, must have seemed like an answer to a prayer, or a dream come true. Only an accident could make such a charity possible. My mother and grandmother had no other qualifications for assistance, unless it was my mother's marriageability, but she was not ready for marriage, and there were no suitors who represented instant security. My grandmother could go to work, but she hadn't worked outside the home in twenty years, and she needed time to pull herself together. Certainly the money itself wasn't all that important—in fact, that grand sum was banked at the time for my mother, who only received it years later when her mother died; but the psychological easement of the money, the care and attention it represented, had to make a difference. And the money's source, I believe, had some bearing on the future for my mother and grandmother; that is, a rich savior was implanted in their imaginations. For what it may be worth anyway, my grandmother went to work for a rich man and my mother decided to marry one. In fact, my mother would never be involved with a poor man, and when my grandmother was through working for her rich man, she bought a house and a lot of antiques. At that point the two women colluded in upgrading their situation as a new trio with me as my mother's replacement. Some tacit decision must have been made after Frederick Crowe died to try out a new kind of family—one without men. But a man of some sort was required to explain the presence of a new addition in their life, and the choice of a dead man for this purpose was advantageous on two counts: he could be anything they said he was, and he would never have anything to say about it.

My mother's program to marry better than her mother had was undermined by her inner certainty that no man could be as good as her father. This posed a contradiction, which she resolved by an ingenious lie: she found a man who was too good to be true and then told the world he was her dead husband. The way she did this was by traveling far enough away to make her story so exotic as to be credible. A "dead" husband would have to be left someplace where the people who knew my mother would most likely never have seen her married. In those days people traveled slowly by boat, and if they crossed the great water in one direction or the other, they were apt to stay. Actually, it would not have been necessary to go very far to have a mysterious relationship. None of my mother's immediate family traveled farther than places like Asbury Park in New Jersey. (My cousin Eddie went there sometimes to play golf.) Even so, a foreign husband would present the most reassuring enigma. And more important, perhaps, than my mother's immediate family was the world at large—her family may not even have presented a problem. Certainly her mother was no problem. Either she was her confidante, or she would accept anything she was told for the sake of a grandchild. Having me was the one thing my mother did for which she was never criticized by her mother. And considering that it was the only thing my mother ever did that *she* seriously regretted, it seems plausible to speculate that her caper abroad was planned entirely to please her mother. Whether it was or not, the two of them had a disagreement as grave as the one her parents had had: if my mother was implicitly charged with the responsibility of bringing back a child, she resented the manner in which she had to do it. It was not having a child that she regretted—on the contrary, she very much wanted one, she always said—but she had never fancied herself alone with one. Much as she was driven for inner reasons to have a child the way she did, she was in conflict with herself from a social point of view. It was not that she believed implicitly in the social order, but once she realized that the social order would not accommodate her, she believed she had made a mistake. She never thought it all out. So long as she conformed, she had no reason to think about the social order at all; only by opposing it would she become aware of it. And once she came to know what it was, she conformed with a vengeance. One can imagine my mother after her father died drifting along unconsciously, yet unerringly, toward her destiny of collision with herself. She wasn't drifting along with nothing to do—not by any means, she was very busy—but her mind was much less active then her hands and feet. She was an excellent student, but she wasn't trained to think or to ask questions or to raise issues. And her ambition to go to college wasn't strong enough to transcend her means. She had a good friend who went to Smith and who wanted my mother to go along with her, but my mother thought she was too frail physically to work her way through. My own interpretation is that she chose something to do instead that would give her an excuse to travel as soon as possible.

At twenty my mother entered nurse's training at Roosevelt Hospital in Manhattan. For a girl who thought she was frail, she chose quite a demanding profession. She did find the work hard and she often said she disliked nursing, but she quickly discovered aspects of the profession that agreed with her or were at least tolerable and sometimes romantic—for my mother, as a nurse, the romance of people and places was more important than the idea of service. In other words, nursing was not her calling, but its fringe benefits were appealing. She was perfectly conscientious and she depended on working long hard hours to keep her mind off her troubles (an addiction I believe she gradually acquired), but she hadn't been loved well enough to display the compassion and care that makes nursing more than a job. Ideally she enjoyed nursing in the capacity of a companion to interesting people who had something to offer, in addition to a salary. For five years during her thirties she worked at the Waldorf-Astoria, where she attended plenty of interesting people, or people who made her job interesting because they were rich and important. But she was a typical nurse who secretly hoped to marry the handsomest doctor and/or perhaps have an affair with a rich important patient. So far as marriage was concerned, my mother was in a bind: in addition to her complex over her father, she had not been trained to serve a man as a wife. If she hadn't been loved well enough in one sense, she had been loved too well in another. Her mother had fussed and hovered over her physical needs and her appearance while neglecting her emotional life. As a result, she was too self-centered on the one hand, and too constricted on the other, to either nurture a man's ego or take care of his domestic needs. But since women generally attempt marriage whether better or less well prepared for it than my mother, I think she would have tried it too, had an opportunity presented itself. As an only child in a family in which her own needs were considered at least as important as her father's, she could easily not have realized what it meant to be a wife. At any rate, she always said she had wanted to marry, but her choices were too ambitious. Her instinct to marry rich was consistent with her pampered upbringing but incongruous with her class. She had the interests of a leisured class without the inborn manners to go with them. Besides traveling, she loved reading and painting and playing games and riding horses. Her manners were extraordinary but exaggerated, and limited by her subversive need to express herself. The air, the hauteur, the detachment—the ability to make small talk meaningful and more personal transactions playful and objective—were missing. Nor was my mother cunning or hypocritical, except in the deep sense in which her inner life never informed her active involvements; or rather she never connected the two. Moving out aggressively into the world, she had few resources for controlling things once she encountered her emotional objectives. Her first job after graduating from Roosevelt Hospital was in Nova Scotia, and within a year after that she went to Paris. My mother had two excellent friends, the Platt sisters, who were like guardians or godmothers to her and who were very important in her life. They were both nurses, just then working at the American Hospital in Paris, and it was at their urging that she went to France. Later, Dorothy, who was the elder of the two, helped my mother bring me to America. She traveled from Shanghai to London to do it, as by then she was working at the American Hospital in Shanghai. Once I asked my mother if she had ever thought of bringing me up in Shanghai instead of America. The idea intrigued and surprised her. Dorothy always sent exotic presents from China: a white silk dress, I remember, and an embroidered jewelry box. Eleanor, the younger of the two, was responsible for the six years I was to spend in an exclusive boarding school where she was the nurse. Eleanor and Dorothy both had huge bosoms and thin stick legs, and Eleanor in particular toppled forward precipitously when she walked. Their brother Norman was one of the men my mother thought she should marry before she became maritally ambitious. Norman let me sit on his lap when he drove his car and I was very small. Eleanor and Dorothy never married, and I don't think Norman ever did either. My impression in retrospect is that the three of them were virgins. I think of the Platt sisters as unwitting intercedents in my birth. Had my mother not joined them in Paris when she was twenty-five, she would never have met the man she chose to be my dead father.

My mother met this curiosity in passage from France to America. It was her first and only European romance. Five years had elapsed since her father's death. It's practically impossible to imagine my mother returning to work in America without a serious romance on her checklist, if for no other reason than that she had long legs and a brilliant smile. Something had to be conquered, and a trophy brought back. On shipboard certain realities are suspended. A passenger ship at sea is a powerful symbol of romance: single women aboard one seem almost proverbially vulnerable. But my mother was already dreaming. The ostensible reason for this return trip to America was a job accompanying a patient to Boston. The real reason was that she was father-bound. Had she been bound for mine, it's doubtful she would have met him on a ship. The exercise here was a double indemnity. By substituting my father for hers, or vice versa, she would secure herself against the loss of either one. Thus, in her mind they were already lost, and the choice of a strong paternal figure, successful and overwhelming and old enough to be her father, was a bid to leave them that way. Her daughter would be a mute ally, whose common plight would further justify her position. The emotions left unresolved over the death of her father were not taken into her calculations: one purpose of a romance with a stranger is to obscure certain memories that a stranger evokes. True to the regressive aspect of these myths, the meeting involved a mistaken identity, which was thrust upon my mother by the captain. Wishing to please an important Englishman on board and a business companion, the captain seated my mother at table for dinner with them. The reason he chose my mother, according to her, was that her name was Crowe, which was confused with the name of a famous actress, Jane Cowl, who was thought to be aboard. I never asked her how the mistake was straightened out, or whether the actress was really on the ship (and perhaps ill) or not, but being cast in the role of actress was like two removes from reality, the better to appreciate a scenario that was already unreal. Yet my mother was not an actress in any sense at all, and her thrill at being mistaken for one was apt to imperil the value, however slight, that she placed on her own identity. Ironically, the illusions such mistakes and transferred values create often serve to further some intimacy that illusions are designed to protect. The actress who knows she is acting will not contaminate her act by believing in it. Alas, though, my mother was chosen to play a part that already involved her emotions and merely provided an excuse to act them out.

One can imagine her dazzled by this Englishman whom the captain wished to impress. She had never met anyone like him before—he conformed to some romantic ideal of an

English lord or prince: he was tall, lean, handsome, amusing, and debonair. "Debonair" was her favorite word to describe him. She remained entranced all her life by the image he cut in tails and white tie when they went dancing at Ciro's in Paris. To a country girl from a dull, plain ("uninteresting") American family, he was the essential stuff of English fairy tales. Assuredly he looked grander to her than Edward VIII did to Wallis Simpson, an affair, by the way, that my mother followed closely when she was in her thirties. It's fair to say that my mother had a common female affliction of that time: the Prince of Wales fantasy. However, the social gap between my mother and father was far greater than that between Edward and Mrs. Simpson. What, then, did this man see in my mother, a mere nurse accompanying a patient to Boston? He saw, for one thing, a version of his younger sister, the woman my mother always told me was crazy (his sister and my mother were both tall, lanky brunettes). She was as close to her brother in her way as my mother had been to her father, but while she was the underprivileged sister, my mother was an indulged only child. This was a privilege of sorts that could make her opaque to her sex–class disadvantage. It could also make her seem wilder and more untamed to this Englishman than she was. She would certainly personify for him the for- eign concept of a young country, still artless and ingenuous. He must have been enchanted by what he perceived as my mother's American qualities. He was having a very successful romance with America, and my mother was a kind of token of the esteem with which he was regarded here. He was a late American invader, but it was not exactly his plan to marry her (America). He took my mother seriously enough to want her for a mistress, but it's doubtful that even an American of Mrs. Simpson's stock would have suited his needs for a wife in England, any more than Mrs. Simpson suited Edward, considering how he was run out of the country because of her. Either he was smarter than Edward, or he was fortunate enough not to fall so deeply in love. In Edward's case, love was a means of abjuring his responsibility, while in my alleged father's case, love was an adjunct to his American adventure, and marriage a means of enhancing his position in England. Some men have more to lose than a crown. This man was building a fortune in England before the actual collapse of the Empire, and his big market was in America. He was not so young when he met my mother—he was forty-one, in fact— and when I was born he was within a year of the age my mother's father had been when he died. For this reason, no doubt, my mother always thought of her Englishman as belonging to her rather than to me. For her he never became a reality as father to her child any more than he did to the child, and in later years she was actually affronted by my curiosity about him. The offense, of course, was due to her sensitivity regarding her social status, but perhaps her social sensitivity and her possessiveness were the same thing. She was just as reluctant to talk about her own father. Quite plausibly she never thought of her father as her mother's husband, or that is to say she never perceived them in relationship apart from her. It was unlikely, then, that she would ever imagine a relationship of mine that was exclusive of her either. A corollary supposition is that her own relationships with individuals were less real than imaginary, thus providing a strong base for possession. My mother never attained a perspective on her immediate family that would permit her to get close to them. She kept them close to her in her imagination, nurturing herself on the fantasies such relationships breed and entail —while she negotiated her survival alone in the world. I was her fantasy child, an appendix to her father, alarmingly real in terms of responsibility, but present only to feed her emotional needs, somebody who was as distant from her as her father really had been but who, in her imagination, was hers exclusive of her mother. Distance is maintained, paradoxically, by symbiosis. The distance she traveled to meet my father, whom she never had the opportunity to know as a person, was appropriate to her development. The distance she felt forced to put between them after she had me always seemed to her like a cruel turn of fate, an event over which she had no control. Unquestionably the initiative was his, but his initiative and her passivity were twin aspects of an emotional position she was not permitted to outgrow. A chance encounter on an ocean liner provided the occasion for updating her fantasy. Essential to its completion was a grand sense of disappointment. The event that clinched this was my birth.

My mother always said she wanted me, and never seriously entertained aborting me; it was her rejection of an abortion that brought about the end of her romance. Her Englishman apparently was adamant on this point, and prepared to provide the most expensive and comfortable abortion available on the continent. My mother just as adamantly refused to take him seriously. On the contrary, I'm certain she nursed the popular fiction that a baby would cause him to want to marry her; marriage, she thought, after a four-year romance, was definitely her objective. She was approaching the great age of twenty-nine, already past the age a female was considered "on the shelf" so far as marriage was concerned. Apparently she thought this was her last chance (after four years of seeing him), and in any case she would never again find anyone as special as this man. But either he made it clear that it was not his intention to marry her, or she divined his intention and applied the pressure of her condition. It's conceivable also that his unwillingness to marry her enraged her, and she reacted by trying to embarrass him. Or she was calling his bluff. Or all of the above. Once pregnant, my mother took up residence at a discreet distance from her objective, in Worthing, a seaside resort town near Brighton on the Channel. She loved the sea and lying in the sun, and she had one friend in England called Sybil. To deliver me she moved even closer to Finchley, a suburb of London. By then it would have been evident that her ploy was not going to succeed—the man in question had made good his threat not to see her again if she fulfilled her term. After my birth she retreated with me back to Worthing to await a possible change of heart. I remember Worthing as a snapshot of an adorable fat baby sitting on a stone-strewn beach. Next there's a series of shots on the S.S. *George Washington* crossing to New York: I came to my mother's country on the first American president. My favorite snaps were those taken of me in a deck chair in the arms of an obliging British sailor no more than seventeen who held me close against his radiant smiling face. In America my mother took me to her aunt Molly's house in New Jersey where I sat contentedly in a carriage wearing a white woolly angora beret. Within the year we were back in Europe, lying in wait on the continent for my father to come to his senses, as is said. Possibly when she saw her mother in America after arriving home with me she was struck by a certain feeling of incongruity about a new trio consisting of three females. Perhaps too at that moment she saw with a frightening clarity that she herself must play the part of father if no one else was forthcoming. On this return trip, however, she stayed away from England and we traveled in France and Switzerland.

For five years we wandered picturesquely around America and Europe but principally in America. In Switzerland we stayed on Lake Geneva at the foot of the Jungfrau and in France in deep snow somewhere in the country. My mother knew Geneva because she had climbed the Jungfrau when she was employed at the American Hospital in Paris. I remember it as a snapshot of a gaily smiling one-and-a-half-year-old, naked and shadow striped from the bars of a hotel sun porch, a view of the mountain off in the distance. I remember being in deep snow somewhere in France, bundled up in a sled with white-mittened hands sticking straight out of a mound of white blankets, forbearing yet consternated. I have no idea whether or not my mother made contact with her object during this time; I do know she was receiving an allowance of some sort, because she wasn't working and because after I was five I found a British note in one of her steamer trunks in my grandmother's cellar. Soon she decided nothing was to be gained by staying abroad and we made our second and final crossing to the States. In a photo of my mother holding me on deck in a small crowd of other mothers and children, we look like well-heeled immigrants. My mother was smiling for the camera as always, belying the great anxiety she felt about her new situation. At the same time, I know she found me quite a satisfactory baby, the trophy she had won as consolation for her loss in the battle for a father. She was, in a way, especially pleased to have a girl. She claimed to have wanted a boy, but actually she preferred girls. (I find it difficult to contemplate my survival had I been a boy.) Anyway, she had me, and the man who refused to be my father was dispatched as dead. Dead was bad, though that was a judgment she would never have applied to her dead father, however terrible she thought his loss. But if the father she chose to be mine had really been dead, she might not have thought he was bad either. As it was, since he went on very much living and he was not living with her, she was naturally inclined to think badly of him; but her bad thoughts about him never affected her opinion that he was the best that could be had. Or rather, had she not thought he was the best, she would naturally not have had cause to be so angry when he rejected her. Unable to think badly of her own father, in this transposition she could mobilize a belated anger. But while her anger was mobilized, it was never discharged, or associated with its point of origin. Here her case rested.

Her legal position, in any case, seemed too precarious to risk a confession. Once in America she became a widow, a woman who should be sad, not angry—emotions curiously interchangeable. I remember her sad, never angry, except indirectly when she was impatient or irritable. I remember nothing of how she was during my first five years, only her image in snapshots, pleased to be my mother, always regarding me with possessive pride and pleasure. She was a glamorous-looking young mother, tanned and slim and stylish. Having breakfast in the sun on Nantucket, she beamed over me drinking a glass of milk in a sunsuit. At my third birthday party on Eddie's lawn in Great Neck, Long Island, she watched happily as I held up a doll in a white cap and sweater that she had knitted for the occasion.

But sometimes she was missing and I was left with strangers or friends. When she was missing she was ill. Once she left me with her English friend Sybil in Paris, once at a kind of orphanage nursery school in Geneva or France. In America I stayed with her friend Bertha Hatch in Pelham Manor, New York, and at another time with a woman called Auntie in New Jersey who took in children whose mothers were sick or working or somehow absent. I have vague unpleasant memories of Auntie, of having mumps and whooping cough and a case of impetigo there, and a great fear of thunderstorms. Bertha Hatch on the other hand was a close friend who loved my mother and had a wonderful house in Pelham Manor. I remember trying to tie my shoes there, and feeling desperate when I had a bad cold and Bertha forced Vicks up my nose, and sitting in a white dress and white shoes in a gravel lane with a dressed-up little boy. Bertha also had a wonderful house on Swan's Island in Maine. This was my mother's favorite retreat. Bertha's little antique clapboard house sat on a rocky cliff facing the sunset, and she had a black sheep and a spinning wheel and a grandfather's clock. My mother loved swimming in the icy water of the cove below the house, and I liked climbing on the rocks and watching the sheep and seals. At that time my mother had another friend called Mrs. Lovelace, who was divorced or separated and lived with her son Burnside. Mrs. Lovelace owned a house on Nantucket where we were also welcome. Burnside Lovelace was a very disagreeable little boy—he was tall and mean and skinny and his knees were knobby. He liked playing a game called Want It—Can't Have It, in which he would offer me something nice but never give it to me. In the photos he always appears with me on swimming docks or in sailboats. I looked up to him, hoping he really liked me no matter what he did. I barely remember Bertha's nephew Little Bill, who was relatively much nicer. Little Bill's mother, Brownie, was Bertha's sister, and her husband, Big Bill, was an accountant who helped my mother straighten out her finances when she was in her forties. Bertha and Brownie were daughters of a man named Rufus Hatch, who had lost his fortune during the Depression; through his daughters he was, in a way, one of the rich men my mother collected. Another rich man was one Mr. Barbay, for whom my grandmother worked in New York while my mother was wandering around the world with me. My only memory of my grandmother before I was five is of visiting her at Mr. Barbay's house in New York and having a torrential nosebleed all over the bed sheets. The purpose of her having this job, apparently, was to save enough to buy a little house in order to help out my mother.

When I turned five, my early nomadic life with my mother came to an end. My grandmother bought a house in Little Neck, Long Island, where I could live and go to school, and my mother went back to work. I became my mother, and my mother became her father who would support me and *her* mother. In the reconstruction of their original trio, only my grandmother retained her identity.

2

The Right Secrets

In her role as father, my mother was much more independent of her mother than her father had been. In a way she was like a divorced husband providing child support and paying regular visits home. During these five years she worked at the Waldorf-Astoria as the hotel nurse, and most weekends she came home, but when I was old enough, sometimes I went to see her at the Waldorf. The winter I was eight I went to Florida with my grandmother. The reason given for the trip was that the climate would help my grandmother's arthritis, but I believe the real reason was that my mother was enduring one of her severe depressions, and if I was away, her own absences could be left unexplained. My grandmother certainly suffered from arthritis, but that was the only time we or she ever went south, and during this period, when I grew from five to ten, my mother worked fairly consistently at the Waldorf-Astoria, but my grandmother always feared she might not, and though she had some money of her own and her home was hers, she was no longer working, and essentially she was keeping house for both of us. Her fears about survival were easily transferred from her dead husband to her daughter, whose weaknesses she knew only too well. Yet unlike her father, my mother had a secure profession, which, coupled with her absence from home, made her less vulnerable to her mother's criticism than her father had been. Also there was a vein of sympathy and under-standing between them, unacknowledged and untapped as it was, that served them both better than the lack of sympathy between my grandmother and her husband. In this updated environment, I was naturally better off than my mother had been in the original model. Certainly I was handicapped by the lack of a father, but there was a trade-off here between a missing father and the greater security they were able to provide without one. This is not to say that my mother gave up trying to obtain a father for me—indeed, the depression she suffered when I was eight was over another man—but her choices and their results indicated that she really preferred her independence to the uncertainty of involvement with a man. She also preferred to suffer emotionally rather than risk the security of providing for herself. In my mother's setup, practical security and emotional fulfillment seemed like mutually exclusive objectives. Yet clearly in both respects she did better than her father ever had. And as an absent father she was more reassuring than the father she herself once had at home. The constant tension that my mother had once experienced between her mother and father became for me only a weekend experience.

My mother's visits home had a whole shape to them. At first she was delighted to see me, and she would pay her respects to her mother and the three of us would have a civil dinner together. Then we played card games and all sorts of other games, and on Sunday morning I would get into her bed and look at the photos in my baby album with her. Looking at pictures and playing games were the things we liked doing together best. I always forgot about the worst parts of her visits, or imagined that next time would be different. I adored her the way she once had adored her father, the parent most esteemed for his remoteness and position in the world. The onus of socialization was once again on her mother, and the role my grandmother played for me was the same she had once played for her daughter. Frequently when my mother was home she confused our names and called me Olive and my mother Jill. In this new version of their trio, my mother was paired off even more decisively with me than she had been with her father. Since I was hers, after all, and not her mother's, I was ideally suited to be her ally in the continuing struggle with her mother. To me she communicated the same sort of thing about her mother that her father once had to her: that her mother was ignorant and difficult. Mainly these communications were atmospheric rather than explicit. I was a witness to their arguments and I remember only my mother's side of them. My mother took the offensive on two accounts, but it was her defense against her mother's questioning that ultimately roused her anger. On the offensive, she picked on her mother for her housekeeping habits and manner of speech. I remember my grandmother doing nothing so much as house-keeping—bending over the tub washing sheets, or the ironing board ironing even the towels—but she was not scrupulous and compulsive like her daughter. It irritated my mother to find dust anywhere or a pile of anything (such as ironed and folded sheets) not yet put away. Spots or dust or any kind of disorder unnerved her. One of her favorite rituals was wrapping up all the winter clothes every year against the summer moths. Packages of woolens were wrapped very neatly and tightly with mothballs in newspaper, then bound with string, identified in ink or pencil, and stored in a sideboard bureau. For years afterward I thought all my clothes would have holes in them at the end of the summer if not stored in mothballs. This was one of the chief maintenance rituals my mother and grandmother shared. They also shared a massive preoccu-pation with their bowels, typical of their class and times. Their goal was to eliminate daily, and any failure of the body to discharge this essential function was regarded as a calamity. As a result, they often succeeded in convincing themselves that they were constipated, a self-conceived and self-perpetuat-ing disorder. In the end, my grandmother died of cancer of her bowels, and my mother was unable to eliminate without artificial aid the last twenty years of her life.

Not surprisingly, their attitudes in regard to discussing sex were also the same. Sex was never mentioned except indirectly and provocatively as something that was either dangerous or not nice. Shame and modesty were taught through embarrassment: the body and its functions were not acceptable in a natural state. However, innocence about sex, like colloquial speech, was one of the things my mother attributed to my grandmother's ignorance. According to my mother, my grandmother had been entirely ignorant of sex before she married and perhaps even afterward. She said her father spent his wedding night in a hotel room in Yonkers sitting in a chair. She said also that her mother knew nothing about birth control and had never heard of homosexuality. Whether these things were true or not, I have no doubt that my grandmother was pure about sex in the old-fashioned sense; that is, she was a virgin when she married and she would never have considered sex in an unmarried state. Therefore she never had another relationship with a man after her husband died.

My mother was a "modern woman" by comparison, but she too was a one-man woman in her own determined way. She never whored so far as I knew, or she was a whore only in the ancient sense of being an unmarried woman. In any case, sex was a source of conflict between my mother and grandmother. If my mother thought my grandmother was ignorant, my grandmother suspected my mother of being indiscreet, though she would never have confronted my mother directly; in fact, she was probably unaware of her own suspicions, and my mother after all was too old to be questioned on this score. But if my mother had been foolish enough to have a child without a father once, why wouldn't she do it again, my grandmother might inwardly reason. The thing was that sex and its consequences were a taboo; thus what might have been aired and dealt with realistically was filtered through channels of silent mutual distrust. The sexual ignorance ascribed to my grandmother was one of my mother's defenses against her mother's knowledge. Her other defenses were not so harmless or patronizing. Anything my grandmother wanted to know was construed as a veiled attack on my mother's lifestyle, or a lack of confidence in her ability to survive and support the three of us. And of course their exchange was very one-sided: the one who had nothing to tell wanted to know what the other one was doing in the world. There was no intelligent conversation between these two women. All matters of interest to either of them that they were able to share remained invested with their survival anxieties. And not least of these matters, of course, was I. My grandmother's fears for my mother in the world were easily matched by my mother's misgivings over placing me in her mother's care. On her weekends home she was confronted with these two impossibilities: her mother's suspicions, and her own contempt for her mother. Late Sunday morning she could be seen lying on the couch in the living room with the back of one hand resting on her forehead, or she could be heard upstairs retching over the toilet. By then our pastimes had been exhausted, and the goodwill she really felt for her mother was spent too. And besides, she had to return to the world, which was always full of difficulties. Her headaches punctually preceded her bilious attacks, a somatic expression of ill humor centered in her liver, which had been damaged by hepatitis and jaundice when she was eighteen. Imitating her liver, perhaps, her habit when her anger finally surfaced was to disgorge herself from the house. By the time she was ready to return to New York at the end of a weekend, she had set the stage for her emotional payoff: her favorite way to leave the house was to storm out the front door without looking back, proclaiming that she would never see her (her mother) again. Then of course she would always see her again the following week—she had to see her to see me. And when she returned, she was delighted to see me as always, would pay her respects to her mother (as though nothing had happened), and the three of us would have another civil dinner together.

We sat at a big round mahogany table draped in a white tablecloth, with a felt cloth protection underneath. My mother and grandmother sat facing each other so I was between them, facing the empty fourth place. The empty man place in our lives was occasionally filled by several ciphers and by my cousin Eddie. My mother's father and mine, of course, were purely historical, hers depicted in her childhood photo album and mine in a book that featured him in connection with his business. Her father was also on the wall in a formal photograph of him and my grandmother flanking my mother as a baby. (My mother had one photo of my father, but I didn't see it until after she died.) I frequently urged my grandmother to tell me the story of how she had met her husband, Frederick Crowe, in a boardinghouse in Manhattan. This was the only family story she ever told me, and I never thought of asking her for more because I had no sense of history apart from what I already knew. It never occurred to me, for instance, that she had had a mother and a father, because she never mentioned them. Of my grandmother's three sisters and a brother I knew only one sister—my great-aunt Mary, the mother of Eddie. And besides Aunt Mary and Eddie, I knew just two other maternal relatives, the daughters of my grandmother's sister Maggie. The reason I knew them, I assume, is because their family arrangements were as unconventional as ours. Eddie never married and he lived all his life with his mother in Great Neck until she died. Martha and Elsie, the daughters of Maggie, never married either, and they lived together all their lives in Queens. Martha worked at the telephone company in New York and Elsie stayed home and kept house for them both; Martha was round and jolly and Elsie was tall, thin, and worried. When I was older, my mother told me Martha was hopelessly in love with her boss at the telephone company. On Sundays, sometimes, Martha and Elsie drove to Little Neck to take me and my grandmother out for an afternoon drive. On holidays we had enormous meals at their house in Queens. Once my grandmother gave her wedding ring to Martha and then asked for it back again, causing a sort of family feud in which they didn't speak to each other for a long time. Martha and Elsie had a brother whom I never knew, possibly because he was married and had a family and/or he lived too far away. Eddie's brother William lived close enough, but I never knew him either and he too was married with a family.

Altogether in my grandmother's family there were nine men: the four husbands of my grandmother and her three sisters, my grandmother's brother, and four sons from these marriages. Of them all, I knew just Eddie, the son who never married. Eddie was the only man who entered our house other than a steady boarder of my grandmother's called Mr. Shoemaker, and another boarder who stayed no more than a week called Uncle Jack. Uncle Jack was a euphemism for the boyfriend of Mrs. O'Connor, who lived next door with her mother, Mrs. Mooney, and her daughter, Florence, a girl my age. For a time, Uncle Jack provided my grandmother with her chief neighborhood entertainment. It amused her greatly to find him sitting in the Mooneys' living room when she peered through the lace curtains of her own living room across the narrow driveway separating our two houses. I myself was horrified both by Uncle Jack and by her interest in him. I thought he was fat and unattractive, and my grandmother's covert jocular curiosity embarrassed me. Somehow, I have no idea why, Uncle Jack moved briefly into our house and stayed upstairs in my mother's bedroom. Possibly he broke up with Mrs. O'Connor or he liked my mother too and wanted to have them both. I don't know. I was just very grateful when he left. My grandmother, of course, may have been instrumental in negotiating his change of quarters, and if so, her attempts to get a man into the house were pathetic at best. Her steady boarder, Mr. Shoemaker, was a loathsome, depressing sort of man, a man who must have had a life at one time but had

given up and become my grandmother's boarder. There was
no life for him in our house. He came and went through the
front door and upstairs to his room or out to work with
nothing more than a diffident nod and a hello between us.
His room reeked of alcohol and cigars and he was a perfectly
harmless character. I'm tempted to think my grandmother
had obtained in him a ghostly reminder of her dead husband.
He was a similar type physically, albeit a lot unhealthier, and
he was lifeless and ineffectual the way I imagine Frederick
Crowe to have been. At least in his new incarnation he was a
paying customer!

The other men in the neighborhood were hardly more impressive than Mr. Shoemaker. And actually, besides Uncle
Jack, who was just an interloper, there was only one. That was
Mr. Lindbergh, the father of Walter and Mildred, who lived
in the other half of our house. Mr. Lindbergh was a carpenter,
a gaunt tall taciturn man whose only role in our lives was to be
visible sometimes in transit. Mrs. Lindbergh was a very sad-
looking housewife who was not well, and the role she played
was to sit sadly on her back porch with a wan smile and exchange amenities with my grandmother. On the other side, as
I've mentioned, was Mrs. Mooney, her daughter, Mrs. O'Connor, and Mrs. O'Connor's daughter, Florence. Mrs. Mooney's
husband was long dead, and Mrs. O'Connor, like my mother,
was living without one. Next to them in the other half of
their house were Mrs. Nelson and her daughter, Lisa, who
were also living without men. These four halves of houses
made up the perimeter of my neighborhood friends and
acquaintanceships. The entire neighborhood consisted predominantly of Swedish and Irish working middle-class people
whose origins in America resembled my grandmother's. Our
English names and their Swedish and Irish names made
no difference in the common denominator of our circumstances. But there was one clear difference between us, and
that was in the superior nature of my grandmother's fine

decor. However, it was not any Englishness, by marriage or identification, that was responsible for my grandmother's taste. Her sister, my great-aunt Mary, had similar furnishings in her house in Great Neck, and Mary's husband had been a German barber. Martha and Elsie also liked fine things, and their mother, Maggie, had been married to a German policeman. But Mary and Eddie in particular lived very elegantly. Their circumstances were modest, but they made the most of them, or at least Eddie did. The link between our house in Little Neck and theirs in Great Neck, always the grander town, was like that between New York and Paris in the cultural sense. Because we were so close, and Eddie was an unmarried son, around forty-six at the time (just the age my mother and grandmother seemed to prefer in men), he became the sole candidate for a paternal role in my young life.

Eddie was an emissary of culture and a delightful man. He was not impressive by any masculine standards of either achievement or failure, but seemed content living at home and supporting his mother by tuning pianos and teaching. Behind this camouflage he got away with being something of a dandy. He loved nice clothes and beautiful things and bourgeois luxuries. His chief diversion was golf—unless it was a quiet interest in other men, a possibility that became the subject of strong speculation between me and my mother when I was older. We remembered a sailor friend he had called Jack and his frequent jaunts to Asbury Park. But we never saw Jack, and in fact we only saw Eddie alone or with his mother, my great-aunt Mary. Every week from the time I was seven and a half or so he drove to our house in Little Neck to give me a piano lesson. My grandmother had prepared for this by obtaining a wonderful black gleaming Chickering baby grand, which filled half the space of our living room. Every week after the lesson Eddie played pick-up-sticks with me on the dining room table and my grandmother served him some cake. Playing games with Eddie was not like playing games with my mother, who hated losing even to a child. Eddie was perennially good-natured and fun to be around. He had a delicious laugh that issued frequently from his depths and rolled upward effortlessly in contagious waves of mirth. This was a family laugh, which in its Little Neck variety tended more to the raucous and convulsive—indeed, my mother's repertoire included a well-developed gallows laugh. Laughing at ourselves was a family survival trait. This could be cruel and humiliating, but it was also an invitation to be funny. Eddie was funny just because he laughed a lot. He never clowned around or played the fool—he was too proper for that—but he had the makings of a fool. I liked going over to his house in Great Neck better than his visits to ours. He had a Model T Ford with a rumble seat, which was the greatest fun to ride in, and his lawn in Great Neck was an elegant playground of flower beds and arbors and a miniature golf course. His house was tiny and cozy and warm. He was a kind of bachelor uncle delighted by other people's children, or at least by the children of his close relatives. His brother's children were more than ten years older than I was, and I never saw them. I didn't have to share Eddie with anyone. Yet the part he played in my life was not that big. Had he really been an uncle he might have been more of a father to me, but he wasn't involved enough to play that role. He told my mother and grandmother that I was sufficiently talented to be a pianist, but whether I pursued the piano or not was of no particular interest to him. He was too amiable and detached to be fatherly—a father would be either more remote or more attentive. In short, he was not possessive. And I have no memory of a sense of loss when I no longer lived with my grandmother and didn't see him anymore. A man like Eddie was ideally safe from my mother's point of view. While she never became immune to the importance a man could have for her, and thus to the terror of losing him, she was determined to exempt me from that fate. Not a single important man was introduced into my life: important men were dead or mythic. When I did finally meet an important man I was very impressed indeed. But by then I was much too distracted by women to die over such a man. The man in my life was really my mother, who placed herself between me and men at large and in particular, and who even sacrificed our relationship to the cause by trying her best to lose me—that is, by making herself the object of my longing.

The earliest I remember my mother trying to lose me was when we would go shopping together in New York. I had to struggle to keep up with her because she never towed me along and seemed indifferent to my own pace and even to my presence. Sometimes I was afraid I had lost her in a crowd, but only momentarily since I was determined to keep up with her. Possibly I suspected she really did mean to lose me, and if she did, I was all the more determined not to get lost—an intention and a response that formed one characteristic part of our life together. The reason she wanted to lose me sometimes, of course, was that I was a burden to her. I was wonderful as her playmate at home, but I was a burden out shopping in the city. I would then (I assume now) evoke her resentment at her plight as a woman alone with a child, and since she felt it was wrong to feel the way she did, she could only express herself indirectly. On the way to Best's or Saks she would be in a great hurry, focused only on her destination. Then, on the subway or bus, she would suddenly become as inert as she had just been active, and lapse into staring vacantly and rather sadly into space. Upon arriving at a store, the business at hand would make it essential to take me into account, and then she became irritable and short-tempered if I was not as well mannered as she was (and she was effusively well mannered) or if she noticed that I wasn't starched and spotless. Then when the expedition for clothes was over, we would have to have refreshment, and since she liked Schrafft's, which was never inexpensive by her standards, our lunches or snacks were unpleasantly accompanied by her complaints about how much it all cost. Clothes were different because they lasted longer, and my mother even thought it was worth it to pay more for clothes that would last longer. Nonetheless both clothes and food definitely aroused her survival anxieties.

Dealing with her unconscious attempts to lose me, I formulated an equally unconscious strategy for pleasing her by at least losing the clothes she bought me. By losing enough valuable things to justify her telling me that I always lost everything she gave me, at length I had an excuse to lose things by complying with her observation, which then became a sort of command. Two objectives might be realized here: I could survive personally by losing only my clothes, and I could win my mother's attention by satisfying her anxieties about me. Her fear of losing me was naturally an unacceptable wish that could best be satisfied simply by providing a focus for negative attention; one way to survive the threat of getting lost is by existing as a wrongdoer. Surviving as a wrongdoer is itself the subject of a vast literature, to which I add my own story. I was a wrongdoer by birth, by virtue of the wrong kind of birth, but the expressions of wrongdoing that make good stories evolve slowly in the trial runs of childhood transactions. Until I was ten and still under the protection of my grandmother, I was a very good child. I had no reason to arouse anyone's fears because I was not especially afraid of anything myself; I started losing things only when I felt vulnerable enough to imagine I needed help. Then by my demonstrating in a socially unacceptable way that I needed help, my mother's latent fears for me were confirmed. Her primary fear, I imagine, was that she was unable to care for me herself; therefore she was the one who needed help, and I had to figure out how to help her by confirming her fears. By my appearing helpless, others might be inspired to be of assistance. As soon as I left my grandmother's house and found myself in alien surroundings, I transferred my mother's fears to the world at large and acted them out for her. At home with my grandmother, perhaps, I looked too good to be true.

If I was different at all, apart from being a child without a
father, a condition curiously echoed in my immediate neighborhood, I was not that convincing as a girl. I was never
criticized for *not* being a girl, but I was certainly more
androgynous than some, even at an age when sexual identity
is not supposed to have congealed. I liked dolls, but I played
ball and climbed trees more than my girl friends. I liked playing toy soldiers with Walter in his backyard better than doll
carriages on my front stoop with Florence. I loved marbles and
electric trains and I never dressed up in my mother's or grandmother's clothes. I was avid about winter sports and biking
and skating and scootering and careering down hills in wagons.
At eight I was sent to the local ballet school, and at the
annual recital, wearing a forget-me-not-blue tutu, I caught a
draft that made me so ill that my career in ballet was promptly
forgotten. My mother can't have been very interested in it
herself, because I remember that although she came to the
recital, she forgot to bring me a bunch of flowers like the
other mothers, and she rushed up on stage at the end and
pressed a dollar into my hot little hand. Ballet and religion
were two things my mother arranged only because she thought
she should. That same year I was also baptized, but my mother
never hesitated to assert that she was a heathen. Baptism and
ballet were among the many things I endured to please my
mother and grandmother. The only thing I seriously resisted
was castor oil. I went to a dreadful public school where I received perfect report cards in all my subjects and in conduct.
I rarely resisted practicing the piano, and I never objected to
my grandmother's overbearing methods of grooming me and
keeping me looking meticulously proper. I looked very neat
and serious and and demure posing for a photo, seated on our
gleaming black piano bench in long braids and a white silk
dress that my mother's friend Dorothy had sent from China.

I was simply not aware that I was a girl, or that as a result of being a girl anything different was required of me. I might have observed that boys never appeared in dresses and that they were obnoxious at school, throwing spitballs and erasers around the classrooms, but such generalizations were never articulated, and I was too young to make them myself. Had there been boys in my family and I been treated differently from them, I can imagine that I would have assumed I was personally different, not that I belonged to a whole different class—that is, sex—of children and people.

In fact, this is exactly what I assumed when I grew up and mingled with boys and men in the "real world" for the first time. If, for instance, I was ignored in a gathering that included boys, I would think there was something wrong with me personally and not that boys as a rule talked only to each other unless a girl had captured their interest sexually. Certainly in the matter of specific kinds of knowledge and aptitudes I was unaware of being channeled into areas considered appropriate to my sex. Like my mother, I loved books and words, and I faithfully imitated her avowed idiocy at numbers and math. Even under special tutorial guidance I refused to grasp the fundamentals of algebra and geometry. In algebra, X, the fabrication of an unknown, not only stumped me but enraged me. In the end, like most people, I assumed boys were mathematical and mechanical by nature, not by privilege. The possibility that nature and privilege have in many cases merged is a fine point even now way beyond my years. I have no idea what more I might know, if anything, under conditions of (sexual) privilege.

My loss of ignorance regarding my status in the world (as a female) has not increased my knowledge otherwise. I still don't understand X, or plumbing or electricity or physics. But by finding out I was a girl, at least I came to understand myself better. While I lived with my grandmother I had no reason to understand myself at all: the way I was was the way I was supposed to be; whatever was wrong was not yet visible. The life I led was the normal American middle-class life. Every convention was observed, the right secrets were kept, and there were no insupportable problems. To all appearances this seemed like a continuation of the ideally uninteresting family my mother always imagined or hoped ours was. If the only questionable detail was my identity as a girl, my mother had nothing to worry about.

The only thing that worried *me* was my grandmother's health. What worried me mainly was the notion that one morning she just wouldn't emerge from her bedroom and come down the stairs. I was braced for that with the idea that I would immediately summon Mrs. Mooney or Mrs. Lindbergh to come and see whether she was alive or not. I had no intention of seeing her dead myself! My curiosity about death at that time centered around an aversion to seeing anything dead. The closest to death I had come was the news of a lady three doors down found dead early one morning in a pool of her blood on the cement walk near her stoop. I made several trips to the lady's cement walk to examine the bloodstain; I was both curious and afraid. I owned three animals altogether while I lived with my grandmother, and I have no recollection of seeing any of them dying or dead. A terrier I had when I was six ran away a lot, and perhaps that was the end of him. A cat called Wally that my mother brought home from the wine cellar of the Waldorf might eventually have been put away. A canary called Petie who accompanied me singing "The Happy Farmer" when I played it on the piano was not eaten by the cat, but he never died either. I heard about Florence's grandfather, Mr. Mooney, having been laid out in their house after his death, and I was intensely interested in the mass embalmment of Pompeii that I read about in my *Britannica*. The story of Father Damien and the lepers intrigued me too—I had leper nightmares—and I was afraid of thunderstorms and hurricanes. The aftermath of a big hurricane when I was seven turned our neighborhood into a mine field of fallen power lines and a playground of horizontal tree trunks.

But nothing concerned me more than my grandmother's health. She was not really in poor or declining health, but she seemed debilitated because arthritis limited her movements and distracted her with pain. I often saw her sitting on the sun porch rubbing her knees and trying to divert herself by looking out the window watching the meager traffic go by. She loved taking me to New York to Radio City Music Hall, but after a time she never left the house unless a relative came to take her somewhere in a car; on one of our trips to Radio City she had fallen down some subway stairs as I rushed ahead to try and catch a train. After that she negotiated all stairs one step at a time, hugging and gripping the banister. My grandmother was not more than sixty-two when I went to live with her, but I remember her only as an infirm old lady. Her shapelessness and dated Victorian style no doubt contributed to this impression. She played an old-lady role. I never regarded her as a person. She was a grandmother, who seemed to exist solely for my benefit. She did nothing for herself apart from what she did for me and my mother. Once at Christmas, when I became aware that my mother and grandmother were Santa Claus, and some principle of exchange took shape in my brain, I was overcome with embarrassment that I had no gift for my mother. But not for my grandmother. In fact at Christmas my grandmother's stocking was filled with coal, according to some cruel custom of forgotten origin. Anyway, long before I might have had to summon Mrs. Mooney or Mrs. Lindbergh one morning to see if she was still alive, I was sent away to school. Apparently my mother had similar fears for my grandmother. But my mother had never been happy about leaving me with her mother. The excuse to send me away was provided by the war. My mother had joined the army as a registered nurse, and since she thought she might go abroad, she wanted me sequestered in a secure place. Thus our family trio came to an end: my mother went to war, my grandmother stayed at home, and I became a boarding school orphan.

3

A Proper Girl

The first school my mother sent me to was so big and sprawl-ing that I got lost in it. This was my first serious experience of being lost. There were hundreds of boys and girls living in segregated houses on acres and acres of fields and woodlands. I lived in a house in the woods with about twenty-five other girls and a housemother. Our chief pastimes were endless Monopoly games and collecting pictures of movie stars. Luckily I spent only a year there—I did so poorly that the authorities became convinced I would do better elsewhere. One fall day my mother appeared with her friend Eleanor Platt in Eleanor's ancient black car to take me away. By good fortune, Eleanor was the nurse at an exclusive school for girls that had only one girl registered in the seventh grade. I had just finished seventh grade, but it was conveniently decided that I could benefit from going through it again. This was the lowest form. There were altogether about eighty-five girls. I was shorter than my classmate and puckish looking and had arrived after the fall term began, so I was instantly smiled upon as the school mascot. The contrast with the school where I had just been couldn't have been greater; I liked this new one as soon as we drove into the quadrangle, or inner court, around which the red brick structure was built. A few girls were sitting in open French windows reading or writing letters, and the vines covering the brick walls harbored a concerto of singing birds.

The school stood on the crest of a big hill or small mountain commanding the Hudson River and the town of Peekskill. In the center of the inner court was a small rectangular lily pool. The approaches to the inner court were through two sally ports, or stoned arch passages, and crowning the building on two corners were castellated towers. From afar the school resembled an impregnable castle, and from within it was a protective mandala, a fortified womb. I would be safe during the war; in fact I could play war myself on the battlements of a place like this. To our north across an inlet of the Hudson was Camp Smith, which one could see in detail with binoculars. To the west and south across the main body of the river lay abandoned warships abreast of one another. A trestle formed a bridge for trains when they emerged from our mountain and had to cross the water. Whenever a train passed by directly underneath us, all the French windows in the school rattled in their lead frames. A large stone terrace occupied a bluff overlooking the vast expanse of river southward. This was a reasonably romantic environment. By contrast with my grandmother's, it was a fairy-tale sort of setting, resembling more closely the places my mother and I had wandered through before I was five. My mother always loved the ocean or any body of water—her favorite retreat in the summer was Bertha Hatch's cliff house overlooking the water on Swan's Island in Maine. And for me, houses on the water anywhere were romantic reminders of the circumstances of my arrival in America on the S.S. *George Washington*. My arrival at St. Mary's coincided closely with my mother's departure for England on the *Queen Elizabeth*. I went to war in a big building on a river and she went to war on a big boat across the ocean. Her war was a renewed effort to plunder England for the help she needed and mine was an effort to attract enough attention to make up for her absence. Our combined effort was more or less to bring the two parts of our world together again. For myself I now had to fight for love because it was no longer forthcoming from a reliable personal source.

The nuns of St. Mary's provided the resistance I needed to express my rage at being abandoned there. These nuns belonged to a High Episcopalian order called the Sisters of St. Mary's. St. Mary's School was nearly a hundred years old, and the Sisters of St. Mary's also ran a charity school in Valhalla, Tennessee. Seven nuns ran our school in Peekskill with the help of lay teachers who lived in one of the school towers. The rest of the nuns lived a quarter of a mile down the road in the convent where we attended mass every Sunday. St. Mary's was well staffed and equipped; its sports and academic programs were completely representative of the Eastern educational establishment. Its brother school was Kent, famed for its crew and work program, and perhaps for its headmaster, Father Sill. It is one of the ironies of glorified orphanages that the rage of their children is absorbed by excellent diversions. Outlets for rage are also traditionally provided by the repressive function of school regulations. Diverted, or repressed, rage was not only contained but unknown. I have no memory of feeling angry at St. Mary's; I was already well trained in this respect by my mother and grandmother. I never expressed anger, and therefore I never felt it. I only know now that I was angry then because eventually I did express anger. At the time, anger was never mentioned or acknowledged, and, in a way, anything not acknowledged or identified doesn't exist. Humans have a remarkable capacity for denying the existence of the unacceptable. I was a successfully diverted child, but at ten I added rebellion to my diversions. By twelve, I had a fair command of guerrilla tactics. Clearly I felt my existence threatened.

At home with my grandmother I had been a lot more acceptable than I was now with strangers. My grandmother was the best protection against my mother, whose judgment was that our place in the world was too weak to withstand exposure. My grandmother's acceptance of me and of my mother's act in producing me was itself our protection against the world, but it's true too that my mother was my best protection against my grandmother, who treated me as well as she did only because she still had my mother to treat badly. And I was their best protection against each other, an unnecessary security, perhaps, had it not been that they were both required to spend time together because of me. Then all that changed when I was ten. Since my mother was going far away, she made the wise decision to remove me from her mother, whom she knew as a dangerous woman in one of her incarnations, the one in which she felt unprotected herself— that is, the way she had felt when her husband died and left her alone with her daughter. I lost my good grandmother before she turned into a bad one. However, I inherited my bad mother who had been my good mother up until this time. But since she was unable to take me with her, I was mercifully granted a chance in a more neutral zone. Unquestionably I had a better chance away at school than I would have had alone with my mother or my grandmother. I was about to offend both of them; I was older and less agreeable, less inclined to please them if it meant not pleasing myself. I was becoming my age. Had I stayed home longer I wouldn't have been any more acceptable there than I was at school. I left home still virtually a baby, but then I grew up very fast—like a street kid, wily in the ways of the law.

St. Mary's was intimate in size and setting, but its facilities for channeling attention to students individually were the standard ones of rewards and punishments. I learned how to excel at receiving both. In the rewards department I became the school's best athlete. At the end of each year I collected bars and chevrons at the athletic banquet to sew on my navy-blue school blazer. Bars signified first team in team sports or first place in individual sports, chevrons second team or place. At the end of six years both sleeves of my blazer were decorated shoulder to wrist with bars and chevrons. The safest way to go to war at my age was by tournament, with sticks and balls for points. St. Mary's had always been divided into two teams that traditionally took their competition very seriously.

The team that amassed the most points during the year won a silver cup with its name and year burnt into it. I was a Defender and the other team was Invincible, and for two of my years I was the victorious captain. At the athletic banquet I collected the silver trophy along with my bars and chevrons, and during the year I kept the Defender mascot, a huge stuffed monkey wearing an orange and black knitted hat and sweater, in my room, or hauled it off to the fields for important games.

The fields and courts were a ready-made arena for aggression, but not enough to contain my new instinct for war. The classrooms were challenging, but academic honors were won quietly and over the long haul. I was not quiet, and I was too impatient to wait. I could wait for athletic awards at the end of the year because the instant acclaim of a victorious point or match gratified me and filled up the void until then. Also, every point or match won was for the team, even those for individual sports, while academic honors were suspiciously individual. And there was no acclaim from peers for high marks in school subjects. I wanted approval from the teachers, but not so much as to jeopardize my popularity as an athlete. Other than our games coaches, the only teacher who won my serious attention was the history teacher, Winifred E. G. Harper, possibly because she offered a "date cup" in English history when I was a Two—that is, an eighth grader. The winner of a great quiz on the dates of English history had her name and year burnt into a silver cup. But Miss Harper was also more personable and approachable than the other teachers. A tiny attractive woman with an impish smile, she taught her dead subject with flair and good humor. History, in any case, was a subject likely to rouse my interest. As yet I had no curiosity about my own, but the history of the world, even at its most abstract, could be exciting just by association with personal concerns still dormant. For the same reason, perhaps, English was my other good subject, even though our English teacher, Miss Anderson, was uninspiring compared to Miss

Harper. Miss Anderson had taught English at St. Mary's forever. She was a tall, quiet, authoritative figure, who, it was said, lived in the town of Peekskill with a house full of cats. When teaching, she rarely left the chair behind her desk, where she stood with her hands folded at her woollen belt buckle, looking down at us from her drawn-up height with large soft brown eyes that held an air of benevolent and slightly bemused indifference. The classrooms in general appealed to me more as arenas in which to misbehave than as opportunities to distinguish myself academically. However, except for the French teachers, it was impossible to make the teachers of St. Mary's feel bad, because they no longer cared. They were either too old and forbidding, with a gentle sort of dignity, or too young and impassive, with a sad sort of detachment. These women, I believe, were refugees from marriage and the world who had found a haven in a religious school. Miss Sherman, who taught Latin and geometry, went so far as to wear a chapel hat even when she was not in chapel. Like Miss Anderson, Miss Sherman had taught at St. Mary's forever. She was as drab as Miss Anderson, but not nearly so austere or subdued—her style actually was quite outrageous. In her chapel hat and shapeless woollen dresses and lisle stockings and mustache and wispy strands of gray hair that refused to go into her bun or under her hat and with her relentless seriousness, she was a perfect target for fun. Yet her very seriousness and sincerity and straightforward teaching style, and her real interest in her subjects, somehow deterred us from trying to tease her. On the other hand, the French teachers were hopelessly vulnerable. There were two of them during my six years at the school, both Frenchwomen who must have missed home and concluded that Americans, or at least American boarding school girls, were boorish. Of all the teachers and nuns, they were the only ones we pestered and teased to their faces. But the nuns were special targets because they were the ones in charge. My project at St. Mary's was to excel at everything. Since it seemed impossible to please the nuns—I was not religious and I found them difficult to understand—it behooved me to displease them in order to attract their attention at all. To this end I flaunted their rules and challenged their authority. The nuns became a collective extension of my mother, whose authority was now in serious question.

By the time she returned from England, I had made a successful adjustment to St. Mary's. That is to say, the school was now my family, absorbing my primary attention. During occasional visits home to Little Neck, I felt in limbo until I returned to school; I preferred visiting the homes of school friends to staying with my grandmother. My mother's visits to school were not at all like her weekends in Little Neck when she was working at the Waldorf. I wasn't indifferent to her presence, but I was uncomfortable when she came and I avoided or ignored her whenever I could. It's difficult to say how our estrangement actually began—I have no memory of a particular scene or event that signified its onset. (There were *never* any scenes between my mother and me; not until I was over twenty-five did a confrontation occur between us.) Our estrangement in no way affected or diminished our importance to each other, it simply altered the structure of our involvement. I now had a life apart from her, and since her presence threatened that life, I attempted to segregate her from it whenever she put in an appearance. As a result, she went underground in a sense. The school was mine and she was an unwelcome intruder, at least insofar as she seemed to demand more than I could give her. Her implicit demand and my refusal to comply with it now formed an essential transaction between us. Even my visits to her places of work, formerly happy events, were marred by mutual feelings of bad will. When she worked at the Waldorf, I played a version of Eloise at the Plaza, and she loved entertaining me and showing me off there. She still liked showing me off, and we still played games together, but she frequently found me irritating, and I felt unjustly abused by her. At school her presence embarrassed me.

One can imagine my mother returning from abroad empty-handed and in an anticlimactic mood. Her big wartime adventure was over: the thrill of sailing through dangerous waters on a great ocean liner painted battleship gray, of surviving the bombings of London, of secret destinations and unknown hazards . . . but more than these, the anticipation of a rendezvous with my father (he was by then married to a proper Englishwoman by whom he had two children), who might perhaps express an interest in my future, if nothing else—a meeting which did take place, but with predictably disappointing results. She was gone no longer than a year. When she returned, she was stationed at Governor's Island in New York and then at West Point. She was now in her forties, and while she was in the army she had no romantic interest; she had work and friends, and she had me. But she no longer had me as a playmate, or at least not when she visited the school. And since she had no other way to relate to me except to buy me clothes and sew name tapes on them and so forth, she retreated—sadly and angrily, as I found out indirectly through her friends. The way I remember her at St. Mary's is slumped over in the refectory, with a sad expression on her face. The excuse I gave her for her disappointment in me was my new negligence. In my zeal to participate in the life at St. Mary's, I had become indifferent to the state of my clothes or appearance. Or perhaps I had always been indifferent and had only been well turned out because my grandmother groomed me. Or perhaps I knew instinctively that if I neglected appearances, I would satisfy my mother's fear and guilt. There was nothing to be gained at school from looking neat and clean—no awards for the best-kept room or person. There were, however, demerits to be obtained from being disorderly. The nuns and my mother were somehow interchangeable in the role of disapproving authority. If my mother's disappointment in me was reflected in my behavior at school, the school reinforced her negative opinion. At the risk of expulsion, the advantage of this state of affairs was that I had better protection through the extra surveillance my behavior demanded. I was now acting out for my mother's benefit: once she had designated me as bad, it became essential to please her by fulfilling her new demands. A rebellious attitude, in other words, is always a response to a parental order. Obviously she wanted me to think badly of her, thus justifying her own bad feelings toward me. The school was a medium between us, the instrument of authority. My mother's friends were another medium. Through them I learned that I was unappreciative of the sacrifices she was making on my behalf. As a result of the combined efforts of my mother, her friends, and the school, I was persuaded to adopt and share my mother's bad feelings. It was no doubt to compensate for this new identity that I was so valorous on the fields and courts of athletic contest. But besides displaying signs of personal neglect and acting like a gladiator, I had other means of coping with the pressure to be bad. Up front I cultivated a clownish personality, and specifically to satisfy myself, I went underground as a guerrilla. In some respects I tackled the project of surviving boarding school with great spirit and humor.

My attack on the nuns was threefold: I invaded their privacy, I flaunted their rules, and I made fun of them, making up unflattering nicknames for them or using the nicknames they already had. (We called Sister Mary Regina, who was our Sister Superior, Sister Mary Vagina—she was an extremely dignified, handsome woman who walked like a swan gliding on a still pond.) By Catholic standards the Episcopalian nuns of St. Mary's were a worldly bunch. Sister Mary Regina collected silver goblets, which were housed in a big glass case on the Stone Corridor. Sister Mercedes, who resembled an English bulldog, wrote adventure stories for teenagers under the pen name Ivy Bolton. A nun who lived in the convent spent all her time making large pastel portraits. Most of the nuns went on vacations, home or elsewhere, and the nuns at school sunbathed on the tower rooftops. The way I remember them is by some look they had or one thing they did by which I caricatured them. Sister Frideswide always waddled through the corridors intently knitting, the wool and needles and her arms resting on the starched white rectangular bib that covered her plump bosom. Behind her back we called her Sister Fatswide, or Madame Defarge (from *Tale of Two Cities*). Sister Philippa was an old woman whose unembarrassed display of long, yellow, broken teeth adorning her perpetual smile accentuated the deep ruts in her shrunken face. Sister Bonaventura, who was extremely shy, always glancing at you with averted head, blushed bright purple colors in Scripture class when asked about circumcision. The habits of these nuns were distinctive and elegant because of their white wings—sprouting up and away like starched gothic antlers from the cap surrounding the head. When they left the premises of school or convent they pulled in their wings and covered the ensemble with a black veil. Compared with those of other nuns their outfits were aesthetically pleasing, but I failed to understand why they covered themselves up in black, and I was at an even greater loss to comprehend the worshipful object of their attentions. My mother never explained to me why she had sent me to a religious school when she herself was a heathen. I must have assumed that religion was tolerable in a secure and privileged environment. But of course I knew I was there because my mother's good friend Eleanor Platt was the school nurse. I made the religion tolerable by cutting up at services, but I was also seduced by the beauty of the services. The pageantry at St. Mary's was intimate and charming and steeped in tradition. For the Christmas pageant every year, musty, embroidered velvet costumes were exhumed for each girl to wear in her assigned part. The first year I was there I was the Courtier's Page; in my senior year I played King Wenceslaus. The nice girls played angels and shepherds. The nicest girl with the best voice and the sweetest face played the Virgin. These girls were not necessarily religious, but nice girls who were friendly with the nuns and attended extra services were probably religious. Two such girls in my class were selected by the nuns to be sacristans, an honorary and coveted position. I envied them and wanted them to like me, but we belonged to different societies. In a class of just nine or a dozen girls, social divisions are clearly demarcated. There were the responsible, studious ones; the attractive, marriageable ones; the despised, excluded ones; and the troublesome, fun-loving ones. My troublesome, fun-loving partner in crime was a girl called Ursula Burroughs Love. She invaded the pantries with me after lights out to steal food; we went down to the boiler room together to smoke cigarettes; and one late moonlit night, we stole down the gravel driveway to the convent to listen to the Sisters of St. Mary's snoring in their sleep. On another occasion we investigated the bureau drawers of the nuns who lived at the school when they were on "retreat," to see what their underwear was like. The true objective here might have been to determine that the nuns had something in common with the rest of us. I think an underlying objective was to create my own subversive sphere of authority. Certain outrages were perpetrated to observe the effects of such subversion. Once I stuffed the organ pipes in the school chapel with Ping-Pong balls, and once I saturated Father Collard's vestments with perfume before Benediction. One time, after a summer vacation, Sister Mary Regina called me into her office to conduct an investigation into my nefarious activities. The result was that I was threatened with expulsion, but my mother pleaded successfully with the nuns to keep me. Fortunately, the nuns liked my mother and even wanted her to become the school nurse. Unfortunately for my friend Ursula, the nuns disliked her father, who was a drunkard, and they expelled her at the end of our junior year.

Along with Ursula, I had one other outrageous friend at school, and her name was Victoria. Victoria's sphere of operations was home rather than school, and through her I learned a little bit about the world, or at least the world of sex and tragedy and grown-up drama. Victoria's home life sounded like something out of *Peyton Place*. She herself claimed to be having an affair with a forty-five-year-old man. Her sister, she said, had been charged with grand larceny for stealing fur coats in department stores. Her father was in a sanatorium with tuberculosis. Her mother had tried to end her life by asphyxiating herself with car fumes in the garage. Her brother was in a lot of trouble at school. Her stepfather had slept with her sister, and altogether there was plenty of incest. No doubt Victoria told me all these things to shock me, knowing I was completely innocent. I was of course shocked and enthralled. I loved visiting her home, which was a splendid sort of neocolonial manse situated in grand seclusion at the end of an endless winding gravel driveway. I loved being met by the chauffeur at the train station and greeted by the butler at the door. Victoria and I liked staying up all night talking and calling Stay-Up Stan, the All-Night Record Man, to request hit tunes. One weekend, in an effort to include me somehow in her exciting home life and introduce me to sex, she imported her brother and a friend of his from their male boarding school. To please her I climbed into one of the two pink canopied beds in her bedroom with her brother while she frolicked in the other pink bed with her brother's friend. However, nothing sexually serious or nothing sexual at all happened between me and her brother, and we were both wearing our pajamas. At fifteen I still wore union suits and was not even menstruating yet. Nonetheless, it was a great novelty to be in bed with a boy, not to mention being in a bedroom with another girl who was in bed with another boy, both of whom were perhaps actually having sex. As far as I can remember, I wasn't yet knowledgeable about the facts of life, but I have no recollection of acquiring this knowledge at any time. I wasn't sexually curious and went on behaving in many ways like my grandmother's little girl. The appeal of Victoria and her exotic home life was that of a storybook romance rather than a reality to imitate. I loved hearing about it and being as bad as I could without having to do what she (said she) did.

I would never have done what Victoria did exactly because I was a boy myself at that time. My adventure in bed with her brother was more like being in bed with another boy than with a sexual stranger. He was not a man and I was not a girl, or we were both mere children and still sexually undifferentiated. At fifteen I had not yet matured and had no interest in doing so, and when I did I went right on being a boy. The day I began menstruating when I was sixteen I ran down to the soccer field and played a major team game. Unlike many of the other girls, I had no interest in boys whatsoever. In fact, I never thought of myself as a boy *or* girl, but obviously, considering my interests and activities, I was a boy at that time and not a girl. I loved adventure stories and I was in love with one of the girls. The "real" girls liked boys and sunbathing on the tower rooftops and they put up their hair in white socks at night and wrote letters home to their boyfriends. I imitated them sometimes, but only because I wanted them to accept me. I was really a sort of impersonator or impostor and infiltrator. I might join them on the tower rooftops, but I had no interest in sunbathing or getting a tan. All these girls were my mother, who loved sunbathing and getting a tan, and I was their child who loved being with her (or them). I also put up my bangs in bobby pins at night in an effort to be like them, but secretly I wished to be different. I was certainly different in my brush-spit pompadour and straight shoulder-length hair. I was different enough altogether to raise suspicions that I was not another girl like them, and their suspicions satisfied my wish to be different but also made them exclude me on the same grounds. If I had been different and a real boy, either I wouldn't have been there or they would have enjoyed the difference. My need to be both different and accepted was gratified by the two friends I had who were different themselves, and by the one girl I loved who was eminently acceptable as a girl and who loved me too. Of my two friends who were different, Victoria was more of a woman than a girl, and Ursula must have thought she was nothing at all, because she wanted to be like me. Victoria was voluptuous and precociously witty and worldly. Ursula was very blond, without benefit of well-proportioned limbs and features. Nonetheless, she was smart and literary and good at sports. I cared for neither her looks nor her other attributes so much as for her interest in my own person—I depended on this interest, which was close to devotion, to implement my most serious escapades against the nuns. Insomuch as Ursula imitated me, she was more of a boy herself than a girl, and indeed as partners in crime we behaved the way two boys might who found themselves stranded in a pack of girls.

I was now my mother's son in a cultural environment that provided all the necessary trappings for this sort of sexual conversion. In such advantageous surroundings, a mother's son with questionable sexual credentials can practice being a boy away from the corrupting influence of other boys who would treat him like a girl. I pressed my luck as an athlete and a delinquent. To cover my tracks, I cultivated the persona of a clown—as a clown I could count on a certain demonstration of affection. In a completely undemonstrative environment, any show of affection was worth its price in extreme behavior. As a result, I received plenty of attention but without the emotional nourishment that places attention in a context of understanding. The American abhorrence of boarding school is based on this assessment of deprivation. Estates of privilege may be waived in recognition of individual needs. The privileged may enjoy the liberty to forego such estates, but my mother was not privileged; thus she placed education above personal need. In a loving environment, achievement is superfluous; in an achievement environment, love is a reward. Love manifests itself in some concentrated or singular romantic image. Achievement is the bait that love eats. This love, or reward, comes in some disguised, refined version of an original loved one. Its reappearance indicates a failure to enter a loving environment at large—an environment of many loved ones.

St. Mary's was an accredited training ground for society. As a boy I could look forward to some emotional fulfillment if I succeeded in any or all three of my roles. Under conditions of necessity, an idle ball player becomes a serious competitor, a mischievous child a serious rebel, an adored only daughter a serious clown. One of these roles should pay off in some intimacy that would satisfy a need for which rewards, discipline, and laughter were comfortable substitutes at best. In quest of a romantic object (unconsciously), I pursued my roles with art and determination. Returning from vacation at the end of my second year, I was accorded a reputation as an outstanding character. The new students heard about me, and the old students welcomed me with the certainty that I would go on entertaining them. The following year, as a Four, or Sophomore, I was embraced by Victoria and her roommate, Georgia, who were one class ahead of me. At last I became a mascot to two older girls who admitted me into their circle. It was not even necessary to impersonate them in order to be with them—they liked me as I was, evidently, and as I was I remained impervious to any peer pressure to be a girl. In a school without boys this was not so difficult; impostors like myself, in fact, filled a certain quota. Girls like Georgia who were far from home, thus, far from any boyfriends left behind, were not insensible to the consolations of boyish girls. Georgia was my first successful transference. She became the object who made all my exertions worthwhile.

My romance was hardly consummated, but the proper feelings had been invoked. My mother's return from abroad roughly coincided with the onset of my romance. Now my mother's presence would be a serious embarrassment, and she would play a self-abnegating part befitting a mother who had placed her daughter in an environment superior to her own background. The embarrassment she felt about my grandmother was now mine about her as well; the same resentment and betrayal accompanied this new social adjustment. This kind of involvement with unattainable objects was typical of a family reaching beyond itself. A certain secrecy was also essential, to protect feelings that were not so much genuine as hopeful, and also to protect the loved one, whose betrayal is such a necessary evil in these social exercises. The secrecy of my romance was ensured by its antisocial status. Its secrecy was also a kind of insurance against success. Not to acknowledge a longing is one guarantee of its failure to materialize. My longing for Georgia materialized in one sense and not in another.

I followed her around like a dog, and she loved me like an owner, but I never presumed more. If I wanted more I had no conception of what more was; whether she wanted more herself was never known to me. But I was the aggressor, and she set the terms of the encounter. Only one setting provided an excuse for intimacy. In the music room I was encouraged or permitted to lay my head in her lap, a posture reminiscent of the Pietà or representative of more adult efforts to reenter the womb. In any case, we were always accompanied by Victoria, whose protection made this daring exercise possible. It was Victoria's idea to inaugurate my musical education, limited thus far to an uninspiring appreciation course. Under Victoria's direction and Georgia's romantic presence, I learned to pine over the choicest examples of the most romantic classics. Our favorites were Brahms's First Symphony, Rachmaninoff's Second Concerto, Tchaikovsky's Fifth Symphony, Mendelssohn's Scotch Symphony, Beethoven's Emperor Concerto, and all of Wagner's overtures.

Georgia was a real girl, with deep roots in the South, and deep roots anywhere strongly appealed to me. I was already a high flier without a sense of country or borders. Living on a high hill in a castle was like living in an enclave. My American experience living with my grandmother had been brief and inconclusive; my earlier nomadic life with my mother was now, in a sense, resumed at St. Mary's. Living in an enclave is more rooted than wandering around, but no less removed from the life of the people. We were completely aloof from the town of Peekskill, through which we occasionally tramped with a chaperone to go bowling, regarding the town as if we were tourists in a ghetto. At home in Little Neck, I was now stigmatized and ignored as a boarding school girl, and the homes of my friends were equally isolated from society. The rest of my life at that time was spent on trains and in summer camps—camps that were white Anglo-Saxon enclaves for privileged orphans just like St. Mary's. The trains provided our only exposure to life at large. Riding through Harlem, I always pressed my face against the dirty train windows, eagerly absorbing fragments of "real life." To me a real life was anything that seemed both exotic and rooted, and indeed the appeal of Georgia was that she was exotic and well connected. She was American like my mother, but much better connected and more glamorous. Any American girl of means was a girl with a successful father, and of course I would naturally pursue a well-connected father in guise of his daughter. This was what my mother was missing, and she always recognized it when I found it. Georgia and Victoria teased me affectionately and called me William, and Victoria called my mother General Johnston. I pursued Georgia like a boy, and Victoria took me home and tried to turn me into a girl. Near the end of my junior year, when they were both graduating, I wrote Georgia a letter declaring my love, causing her to cool considerably, setting the stage for a retreat more decisive than the contingency of graduation. At that point I had to become a girl, or there would have been nobody to appreciate me. Ursula was expelled at the end of the same year, and none of my other classmates was different enough to make it worthwhile going on being different myself. Neither were any of them exotic and therefore available as new objects of longing. The expulsion of Ursula sealed my fate as a girl. There were seventeen of us left, and while the others were not necessarily girls, neither were any of them boys. The other boys had long since graduated. I idolized several older boys when I was in the younger forms, very dashing girls who were fine athletes. Now my own class had arrived at the top, and I was the only dashing girl under suspicion as a boy. At last I came of age as a girl by falling in love with a real boy in a boarding school like ours.

I say "falling in love," but I was less in love with the boy than with my new status as a girl. I was in love with love, or the propriety of the love object—I wasn't nearly so interested in the object himself as in the idea of him. I much preferred realizing that I had him than being with him; when with him, I was filled with foreboding and uncertainty. I felt constrained to defend my virginity, still a point of honor for "nice" girls, but the required defense opposed an equally pressing demand to please. To remain interesting under these circumstances was an occupation for which I had no training or impulse. Had I simply wanted him, I doubt that the obligatory resistance would have meant that much to me. Had Georgia wanted me, I wouldn't have felt inhibited by the even greater ban against intimacy with another girl. The consequences of having sex with either one of them seem in retrospect as dire as not wanting sex or being able to have it. Nothing was so dire as the issue itself. What I actually did or didn't do was secondary to my emotional choice of sex. A future as a normal girl or as a girl who preferred girls was hanging fire. If there was indeed a choice, as some argue there isn't, given everything that had happened up until the time when such choices were to be made, and if I already preferred girls, as seems likely, the choice of this first boyfriend would be a deciding factor: if I cared enough about him, I might become properly socialized despite my basic preference. I certainly did care about him, but in order to overcome my predilection I would have had to care about him more. Or he would have had to care enough to make me care more; he would have had to care enough, for example, to transcend our separation when we went our different ways after graduation. A heavier relationship than we had was essential to our keeping going. What we had instead was a strong interest on my part in maintaining appearances, and a weakening interest on his in seducing me. He was giving up and I never gave in. On the other hand, I hated giving up the appearance of having a proper sexual object. I clearly had the idea that he was the only proper object in the world, while he obviously knew that there were others, and that another proper object could satisfy his sexual interest. As proper objects go, in any case, I wasn't proper enough. I wasn't motivated enough to please, nor was I glamorous or well born. He was not that impressive in these respects himself, but he was certainly handsome enough, and he went to the right school. Mainly, he was a real boy and he was one of the smart, good-looking, and popular ones: he was the head prefect of his school; he played baseball; and he had a scholarship to Princeton. During my senior year at St. Mary's, I was a model of the best design for a girl. It would seem that my mother's perfunctory efforts to turn me in the right direction had been successful. She never by any means imparted a convincing impression of men and marriage as a goal, but she did feel obliged to point me in the proper direction.

By this time she had long returned from England and her wartime adventure and was now based at West Point, which was only twenty miles or so due north of St. Mary's, on the other side of the river. From her own rocky cliff and castellated vantage point, she tried to exert an influence on my development. West Point cadets were considered perfect for boarding school girls. Having failed to obtain the help she needed in England, my mother launched a new offensive to improve our prospects. Dutifully and with a mixture of breathless anticipation and great fear, I went over to the academy to "drag"—as they called dating there then—in a yellow organdy gown with short tulle sleeves and a square-cut neck. Not since wearing my forget-me-not tutu when I was eight to perform in the annual ballet recital in Great Neck had I felt so uncomfortable or embarrassed. Nonetheless, I, like my mother, thought it was eminently the thing to be doing. While we never said so, we both loved all the braid and uniforms and marching around. In its own way, the academy was just as impressive as the Waldorf-Astoria had been. I had been Eloise at the Plaza at the Waldorf during the five years I lived at home with my grandmother, and at West Point I became Eloise unrecognizable in her efforts to grow up. The best thing available at West Point for an outgrown Eloise was the great indoor riding arena. Times had become more serious. A war was going on, and a future as a proper wife was at stake. On my own turf at St. Mary's, I continued to be as boyish and silly as I pleased; on my mother's turf I had to do what she wanted and pretend to be a sort of debutante. Nothing was quite so stiff and awkward and unnerving as dancing with a strange young man in a crew cut whose brass buttons pressed like cold bottle tops into your chest and stomach and who gazed abstractedly over your head into the middle distance, thinking no doubt about his military exercises or dreaming of a famous movie actress. This indignity was compounded by certain efforts, also considered obligatory by the cadets, to seduce their dates after the dance. Fortunately, I was just as obliged to defend myself, and the worst thing that happened was my failure to view the cadets with the respect that seemed their due.

My introduction to Guy Newland at Kent was a lot more promising. To all appearances, there was plenty of hope. I was developing in two distinctly different ways. The contrary way was visible, but I was only conscious myself of wanting to be socially correct. Yet the contrary part recurred and flourished, despite my best intentions to be proper. For example, I was tall for a girl and I refused to slump. Every proper girl who was tall learned to slump at an early age. At Kent a belated effort was made to initiate me into slumping. The student body tried to shame me into it by serenading their head prefect with a popular advertisement about being "taller, taller than she is" in Adler elevated shoes. The cause was taken up by the head prefect himself on one occasion, when we exited from the dining room and he told me in dire undertones to "get down." I got down and walked out with my knees bent, but I never learned to slump. I did, however, learn to feel tall for a girl. I rarely saw another tall girl, because they were all in hiding or slumping—tall girls didn't come out of the closet until after the fifties. I always marveled at girls who were six feet or over; I thought they were damned to a life of embarrassment and exile. The sure sign of a tall girl was the shoes she wore to help her look shorter. She would be seen slumping in low-heeled ("sensible") shoes and nylons and a white rayon Peter Pan blouse and a Scotch-plaid skirt. Only on informal occasions did she look like everybody else in saddle shoes and penny loafers, or sneakers. "Formal" and "informal" confounded me because I was in school or camp uniform most of the time. I loved being in uniform because it left me free to think about everything else. I hated thinking about clothes at all; I let my mother do all the thinking about them, and therefore I was often dressed in clothes suitable to my mother and not to me. Even the casual observer might have noticed that my mother was doing her best to retard my development as a female. Not only was I tall for a girl, but I was convinced that my mother alone could take care of my clothes. I let her select them and then I frequently lost them. I let her come to school and clean them and pack them, and I let her make me feel guilty for not doing it myself. By carrying on in this manner, I was encouraged to be a boy on the one hand and a girl on the other. Only a guilty mother would continue to pick up after a girl when she was coming of age. Only a girl would feel guilty about having her mother continue to pick up after her. By acting in collusion to maintain me as a boy while cultivating the feelings of a girl, we tried to cover our tracks socially. No girl (not even a girl posing as a boy) could get very far without apologetic or culpable attitudes. My course was truly set. Having a proper boyfriend was mere playacting, but my feelings of loss and inadequacy were very real. After all, I aspired to be a girl, and any failure to be one was cause for remorse. Playacting as a girl was a serious social business. The loss of a boyfriend who was a romantic idea could be as catastrophic as the loss of a real interest—a young girl or even an older girl might not know the difference. The difference might *never* be known. A boy posing as a girl may ultimately discover the difference by comparing his experience with other girls. As a boy I had already discovered that the love of girls was superior to the love of a boy: to a boy I wasn't girl enough, but to a girl I was boy enough to excite her fancy. The peril in each case was that I might become a proper object to some boy, or that I would be uncovered as a girl by a girl whose love I needed. Eventually I did become a proper object to a boy, and other girls never did fail to uncover me. Both eventualities satisfied my mother, who wanted to save me from men but not necessarily from marriage, and whose interest in my girl friends was a front to get rid of them.

In the meantime, I graduated from boarding school in a white gown and a permanent wave, still secure in my Salinger-style romance. I smoked dozens of cigarettes on the train runs between New York and Peekskill, and I met Guy Newland under the clock at the Biltmore. I was still a virgin, but I had undergone my initiation into alcohol and nightclubs and fraternity attitudes. To all appearances it looked as if I was going the way of most boarding school girls. After two or four years of college, I would settle down in Westchester or some other enclave for privileged easterners, raising the children of an educated, ambitious boy. To all appearances I was no longer different. A regular boy had turned me into a girl, and the other girls considered me one of them. However I was not turning into a young lady. I was quite shy and withdrawn, but never demure and flirtatious. I refused to slump, and I never stopped running around like a boy. I still loved competitive games and adventure stories best of all, and I had no interest in clothes or hairstyles or makeup or dancing. I loved being with girls, but as far as I was concerned, I was never really one of them. I had lived among them for so long that I was obviously one of them, but I was just different enough to cause them to set me apart—a condition of special attention, which they bestowed as a recognition of difference. That summer after graduation my double life as a successful girl concealing an adventurous boy split apart. In the space between identities, I became a failed girl. During my first year in college, I entrained into New York from Boston and ritualized my death as a girl by languishing under the clock at the Biltmore. I mourned the death of appearances and the end of being in love with love. The war was over and so was mine in its opening round with society. The struggle for love at college assumed new and subtler dimensions. There was no war at large, and girls were under greater pressure than ever to be girls. The clock at the Biltmore was my personal war memorial. The death of my father, whom I had thought was already dead, was imminent. His business in America was over and mine had just begun.

4

A Father's Daughter

The death of my father was the outstanding event of my college years. The news of his death caused a great shift in my understanding of reality. Suddenly I was no longer simply a girl with a dead father and a widowed mother. I was now a girl whose dead father had really been alive and was now dead and whose mother was a divorcée. The news arrived in two envelopes. I was in college in Boston and my mother was working in Oscawana, New York. In one envelope my mother had enclosed the clipping from the *New York Times* of my father's obituary. In the other she sent a letter rearranging her story to suit this new information. The reason she went to such trouble was that she feared I would see the obituary myself, or that someone I knew would see it and tell me about it. A short obituary in the *Times* changed our lives radically. Had she not feared exposure because of it, I might have remained a girl whose father had always been dead and whose mother was a widow.

Many children of my circumstances are told that their fathers are dead—my mother was as traditional in this respect as in so many others. For all legal purposes, such a father *is* dead, and the truth is considered a threat to the status of both the mother and father and the equilibrium of the child. The mother acts like an adoption agency in her capacity as guardian of vital information. In a sense she adopts her own child, insomuch as she decides to have it and keep it illegally.

She controls information about the father to protect and advance her situation in whatever way she can. Until my father's (actual) death, my mother had going an excellent protection racket. The obituary in the paper provided a masterful opportunity for advancement. In one stroke my father came alive for me and stimulated my imagination. The information I had previously had was impressive but completely inert. When I asked questions I received the same stock replies, and I never consciously suspected that I should know more. I knew essentially four things about him: he was English, he was dead, his business was important, and he had a crazy sister. Now, suddenly, the most striking information about him was under revision. The discovery that someone very close to you who for years you had thought dead had been really alive is amazing news, and I was absolutely amazed. My amazement overshadowed any other emotion. One of the secrets that typically shrouds adoption cases had by a turn of fate been exposed. Now I really wanted to know who he was. I wasted little time going to the Boston Public Library to look him up, and in New York I went to another monumental building where I introduced myself to a man who was intimately acquainted with my father and his line of business. However my curiosity just then was exceeded by my emotional needs, which I satisfied instantly by confiding in one of my teachers. None of my schoolmates was equipped to deal with such a novelty. Their response to my news ranged from blank horror to helpless astonishment, mirroring my own initial reaction rather precisely. As for the teacher I selected to receive my news, I was already madly in love with her. I went directly to her house in Brookline, where she listened with just the right mixture of reserve and concern. Her concern was not the least bit soapy; rather more like a combination of interest and a new regard. Somehow it enabled her to find me reciprocally attractive, thus becoming the basis for a romance in which I could sublimate the whole issue—my mother's perfidy and a father who had died twice. A death and a romance were the outstanding events of my college years.

My new object of longing was as exotic and rooted as the schoolmate I had loved at St. Mary's, and as an added attraction I found her in her natural habitat. I was the stranger as usual, she the exciting native who was here long before me. She was older than my mother and a lot better connected and even more independent. She was not a world traveler like my mother, but she was much more sophisticated. Traveling never made my mother worldly; at heart she remained a naive American country girl. My teacher was a cultured and stylish Boston Brahmin whose family had prospered in America. Her father was an old, retired, white-haired sea merchant. In me perhaps she saw an earlier invader in the form of another father. In her certainly I saw a woman much more masculine than my mother. By that I mean she was worldly and cool and strong in herself. Her style was tailored femme, a style my mother was unable to wear without looking more like a man, or a failed girl, than the wilting femme she really was. Whatever she was wearing, my mother's long legs and aggressive forward stride belied her true emotional nature. Her ready smile and extroverted manner were also deceptive. When her social business was done, she retreated behind her façade in a web of reveries and lost continents; and although she might discuss the events of the day, always aligning herself with public opinion, she was personally opaque and unresponsive to the intimate communications of others. Her recent communiqué to me containing intimate information vitally important to both of us was never substantiated in person. Having just lost my father (again), she now claimed to be divorced, a cue to our ensuing relationship. My mother's outrage in having me illegally had now fulfilled its first term. The isolation appropriate to an act for which there was no consensus, no ideology or platform, had at last cut her off from me too. This was her great opportunity to share the whole truth with me, but she could hardly share a truth that she felt made her culpable in the eyes of the world. What she did share was a sense of her great deficiency: she had mismanaged her information . . . she was very sorry about it . . . she had hoped to protect me . . . it was not her intention to lie. . . . And so forth. Thus setting the stage for the entrance of another mother, one who would deliver me from the curse of my own.

My teacher already liked me. I had excelled at her subject, which was every aspect of dancing, or at least displayed a great deal of enthusiasm for it. I had stalked her through schoolrooms, and had made up countless excuses to see her. I was not necessarily the best dancer in school, but I had eliminated my competition. I was her "pet," in other words, so her receptivity to my "story" when the moment arrived was hardly ungrounded. Then as her interest was activated, I advanced from pet to protégée. She took me in hand and introduced me to culture and the world. She was of course superior to my mother in every way. She wore clothes that looked right on her. She drove a smart Pontiac convertible. She drank Vat 69 before dinner. She lived in her own house with her own antiques. She read things like Emily Dickinson and *Leaves of Grass* and *The Golden Bough*. She had an exciting history and she had exciting friends. One of her friends was the great impresario Sol Hurok, who had actually been her lover sometime during the thirties. Her two closest friends were professional women as glamorous and impressive in their different ways as she was. One was Margaret Lloyd, the dance critic of the *Christian Science Monitor*, and the other a professor of sociology at Rutgers. Her old friends were even more impressive because they were famous dancers and choreographers. She introduced me to her close friends and her old friends as a protégée and ushered me right into their world; I led my life as her protégée in one guise or another well into my adulthood. I followed her old and famous friends to New York after I left graduate school and imitated them by dallying seriously in their field. Eventually I imitated her close dance critic friend and became a dance critic myself. For a while I had a hand in making younger dancers and choreographers famous; then finally I began to make things up on my own and ceased leading the life of an adult protégée.

My teacher was a guide, initiating me into "high" Gentile taste. Her role was something in between mother and father. An introduction to culture, in which my father's identity was subsumed, and which forms a buffer between State and people (that is, the power of the father and those who suffer it), held at least some promise of access to the father world. Anyway I was delivered over to culture, the great realm of paper and performance where our ancestors have taken up immortal residence. Any pursuit of my father at any age when culture was still unknown would have been a disappointing personal exercise. My father was not disappointing in himself but he had gravely disappointed my mother, whose cause I was not yet in a position to betray, much less understand. I entered culture very aggressively, like a boy in a foreign country motivated to survive by learning everything he can about where he is. A country as foreign as culture to a girl like myself was a study of personally unrelated and objective information —all the information was outside myself and unrelated to me. The moment I merged with culture, I found my father there and was then ready to pursue him back to England. Years passed, however, before I merged with culture and had the nerve to revisit the country from which I had been banished. The story of this book is how I got back.

Back in college, in love with my teacher, I was very out-going, though I wasn't going anywhere in particular. The space I was consuming really was that of desire for my teacher, whose attention was the reward that made every activity meaningful. Attention for achievement was at last refined by emotion. A gap was closed between my mother's love and the attention required to make up for its absence. My mother still loved me, of course, but I no longer thought so; that is to say, her fears for me had cast her love in serious doubt. Her fear of what I must have thought about her just then was perhaps the critical emotion coloring her love. This fear has certain aspects of a self-fulfilling prophecy, which apparently involves divorce followed by progress. If she convinced me I couldn't possibly love her, I would find somebody worthier whom I could. This is a very exclusive exercise. I would always hold out for my mother, even while I thought I had disowned her, and she would just as consistently deny her importance to me. Her denial, ironically, was a basis for never letting go. Her fear of what I thought of her was really a fear (a conviction) that others were better. If others were better, I would only love them in reaction to her, and reaction is not an inclusive mode of alliance. Love defined by reaction is a temporary obsession with the better part of a bad deal. Love based on acceptance is a gift of parents who have no reason to compare themselves unfavorably with others—not the form of love encouraged in an upwardly mobile society. In our scheme of things, my mother dutifully played the female part, deferring to male prerogative as the measure of esteem or standard of aspiration. And since there was no male in the family to exemplify the standard, she simply capitulated to the culture at large and let me go. She provided the funds and insisted on the proper educational settings, and I found the models who made her sacrifice worthwhile. She deferred to my teacher as if she were a man, and indeed by comparison she was. As a man she was either a male mother or female father, a familiar mythological figure who does things natural mothers cannot. If I was Hephaestus, the crippled and cast-off son of Hera, who bore him parthenogenetically, she was my Thetis, the goddess under the sea who rescues the sons of rejecting mothers and gives them something to do. Any mother's son born a daughter is a Hephaestus in the patriarchy. My mother was herself this kind of daughter, an only child whose mother had been left by her father, both her own and her daughter's. My mother had her own Thetis in the form of her older friends the Platt sisters, who had encouraged her to join them in Paris when she was a young nurse. Like my teacher, the Platt sisters were childless and they belonged to the world. My teacher had two sisters who belonged to husbands, and she had no brothers, so she was a father's daughter who kept her father's name and internalized his attributes. Her name, by fraught coincidence, was very similar to my grandmother's; both her forename and her initials were identical, a fact unnoted by me at that time, perhaps for the reason that I always called my grandmother "Gran" and never called my teacher anything. But I was not yet in the habit of recognizing such associations, and when I did I saw them everywhere and not necessarily to any purpose. From distance and perspective all significant agents reveal underlying connections. My father had just died and in two more years my grandmother would be dead, and each death was succeeded by a romance with someone old enough to be either and bearing other insignia of the grave and the future. Two deaths and two romances were the outstanding events of my college years.

My second deliverer was exotic just because he was a man, and not only a man but a real foreigner; and he had strong roots in America as well. Like myself he was an English expatriate who had arrived in America on a big boat. Like my alleged father he was English, he was dead, his business was important, and he had a close relative who was crazy. Actually, of course, he wasn't dead, but he was in serious limbo when I met him because he had just been retired. And his wife was not really crazy; she had only been lobotomized at one time. (My English father's sister was not really a crazy person either, only an eccentric—it was my mother's notion that she was crazy.) The English father I met in graduate school was old enough to be my grandfather, but by the most striking coincidence of all in this bizarre case, he was exactly the age my father had been when he died in England two years before. I had no picture in my mind of my father as an old man. According to my mother's original story, he was a much younger (dead) man, as young as her own dead father. Two young dead fathers added together make one old man, a calculation simpleminded enough to seek implementation at some gross level of consciousness. Numbers and names light up our computer boards to let us know that an ancestor is about to put in an appearance. The "ancestor" in question here was totemistic in a general as well as a personal sense.

The setting for his appearance was a seminar on Plato: this old man's specialty was Plato, whom he taught as a kind of ministry. He was terribly impressive. Not tall, dashing, and debonair the way my immediate forebear had been described to me, but short, soft, and slightly round, and very eloquent. Large kindly hazel eyes and bushy brows dominated his open face. He was instantly the most impressive man I had ever seen at close quarters, or at least the first impressive man to appear in my vicinity and notice me. He noticed me the way I imagine a doting father would gaze upon a favored and only daughter. If so, he was twenty-two years too late, and while I fell under his gaze and influence, I was already much too dominated by women to be turned in the direction he represented. I used him, in fact, to make the direction he represented as unlikely for me as when it had been unknown. He was much too impressive ever to be duplicated, and he was old and married enough to suggest that young and marriageable men were not at large. Nonetheless I did eventually get married, but not because I succeeded in locating a model better, or as good as, or even close to the archetype of the old man. Not at all. I got married only because it was the thing to do and I had no idea what else to do at the time. But that happened six years later. It was under the rubric of the thing to do that my philosophy professor seduced me.

Sensing that I had a problem, he presented himself as a father confessor. Already somewhat hypnotized by the intensity of his gaze in our seminar, I had accepted his invitation to tea after class with bated excitement. For at least a year by then I had been rather desperate over the direction my sexual inclinations seemed to be taking me. Innocent as I was, I had not failed to observe that something must be wrong with me if I liked only my own sex. Yet I had no reason to believe I liked only my own sex based on just my experience with my dance teacher. Moreover that one experience was so special and rarefied as to transcend known social values. The object of my love was so much older and established and reputable that, if anything, had I actually thought about it, which I didn't, standard social values would have seemed inverted. I was proud of my affair with a popular and stunning teacher. I was too much in love to care what the world thought and I had no reason to challenge the world either. A secret life that is satisfying gives no cause for questioning values it opposes; such a life that is unsatisfying may give no cause for questioning basic values either. I had no idea actually what basic values were; they were deeply assumed and never enunciated and therefore unknown or unobjectified. But during my second affair, which was undeniably with my own sex once again, and which was unsatisfying emotionally since I was still in love with my first affair, I developed the strong suspicion that I was personally different from the rest of society. This suspicion constituted an educational awareness of basic values, which could be seen in relief to my personal situation. My earlier wish to be different was now superseded by a need to conform. Obviously I was different, that had been established easily, and the more obvious and established it was, the more imperative it became to conform. It was especially imperative when the nature of my difference had itself become divided.

The affair with my teacher in Boston had been a lot more of the mind and heart than of the flesh. My next affair was very lusty and not at all a matter of intangibles. Alas, I was still in love with my lady in Boston while being introduced to the finer points and grosser pleasures of sex throughout a cold winter season on a college campus in Minnesota. At that time such encounters were understood collectively and tacitly to be purely circumstantial. No amount of love and pleasure was likely to withstand the pressure to think straight. My tall handsome lover, who was thirty years old, paid her respects to basic values by hinting that in the future I would be attracted naturally to men. My teacher in Boston had intimated the same by casually suggesting I let my hair grow long and by encouraging me after all to be a dancer.

Unable to wait for these "normal" developments, in the middle of my lusty affair in Minnesota, I put in a desperate telephone call to a male friend in Rhode Island who had been writing letters and poems to me for two years and asked him, ordered him, to meet me at a hotel in New York during Christmas vacation. Suddenly my virginity was a great issue and it seemed urgent to lose it. I had no sexual interest whatsoever in my poet friend, but I was hoping that my lack of interest would dissolve in the urgency at hand. However it did not. I met him in New York at the appointed hotel where, having taken off all our clothes, absolutely nothing happened; more had happened when I was fifteen in bed in pajamas with Victoria's brother. I returned to Minnesota as unregenerate as when I left and went on enjoying myself in the manner that divided me from the heart and split me from society. All of this was about to be resolved in North Carolina the following fall at tea with my philosophy professor. Over tea I told this old man about my dead English father. Then I told him about my misalliances with my own sex. Then he told me there was nothing wrong with loving your own sex—as a Platonist he was in a good position to know. We had just finished reading the *Symposium* in his seminar. No doubt he mistook me for a boy, or he made the best he could of his heterosexual limitations by seducing young girls who were boyish enough to pass. His wife had long turned into a motherly domestic and he hadn't shared a bed with her in years. It's tempting to imagine that had he taught at Harvard instead of Wellesley for twenty-eight years, he might have enjoyed the true Platonic ideal, but obviously he had gone to Wellesley because he liked girls, and he liked them for reasons of class and family background long before he was introduced to Plato. Like my father, he was a late English invader; unlike my father, he came to stay and improve his circumstances.

He was born and raised in a large struggling family in Liverpool who belonged to a Christian sect that provided scholarships to send promising youth abroad for the ministry. At sixteen he arrived in America by steerage with an older brother to study the gospel at a Bible school in Tennessee. At eighteen he returned home to attend his dying father, whereupon he entered the University of Manchester to study theology and prepare for the ministry. At Manchester he was diverted to Plato by the philosopher Samuel Alexander, and he completed his studies at Heidelberg and Harvard. At Harvard he was a student, friend, and protégé of Alfred North Whitehead, and through that association or some other he also knew Bertrand Russell. These names were suddenly as luminous to me as those of the famous dancers and choreographers who were friends of my first lover and teacher in Boston. Everything this old man said and everyone he mentioned had weight and significance. I hung on his words as if they were crampons in death-defying rock-face mountain expeditions. I read the words of his friends with the conviction that they would save my life. I became an avid intellectual. If my first deliverer gave me something to do, my second gave me something to think about. Having played a kind of Hephaestus to my first lover, I now played two female roles in relation to the great Zeus, who traditionally had delivered himself of a daughter just like him to help protect him from the wrath of Hera, his jealous mother/wife. The role played

by young boys in ancient Greece was paralleled and memori-
alized in the birth of Athene, a prototype for certain later
historical individuals who have yet to emerge on the world
stage as a visible group. Elizabeth I is the best known "modern" example of the type. The execution of her mother by
her father gave her the unique psychological opportunity to
rule as a virgin queen. As such, she protected her realm for
her (dead) father. With no apparent realm to protect, I was
about to become a father's daughter myself. The price of this
new estate was my virginity, which I was eager to lose anyway.
The seduction of college girls by male professors was considered a form of guidance enriched by pleasure. Physical pleasure in this instance was nothing but a hopeful by-product of
initiation into the father world. This English father's orientation to pleasure was directed by relief and the demands of his
ego, which was somewhat impaired just then due to his sulky
retirement from Wellesley. He was not a sensualist, and/or
the circumstances of the affair were constrained. Sex was much
more perfunctory than inspired. To a virgin like myself it
represented all there was. It was certainly sufficient to meet
both our demands, his for relief and mine for the association.
Presenting myself as Metis, the secret lover of Zeus, in the
manner of that myth I would allow myself to be swallowed
in order to emerge from his head. To that end he ate me and
entered me and dropped the seed that bore the fruit of intellect rather than child. The loss of virginity per se did not entail
the loss of a virgin nature—losing it to Zeus, in any case, was
a certain guarantee of eternal maidenhood. My lapse into
marriage six years later was a social failure dictated by a convulsive reaction to my mother's final disclosures. My other
encounters with men were those of an occasional whore, never
serious, frequently in reaction to a slight by a woman, sometimes in heat or for lack of the proper woman at all. As for
my professor, I was not that serious about him either. I was
deadly serious about what he represented, and I was quite
fond of him too, but once again I was more in love with love

and the propriety of the object than the object himself. The resolution of my sexual problems at that moment created another more profound and lasting problem. When the affair was over at the end of the year I was successfully reformed, and my interest in my own sex became as furtive and unacceptable as it was supposed to be. I reverted immediately to a choice of this nature, but my choice was suitably difficult to obtain, thus leaving me free to imagine that the only thing missing was the right man. This also left me free to pursue my studies, which had been outlined for me by my two deliverers. Armed with philosophy and geared for dancing, I arrived in New York, in 1953, bound for Columbia to think and the studios to dance. Parallel and separate, over the course of the next four years my two fields of study would merge in a career that combined both but was unpremeditated by either. In dance criticism the professor and the dance teacher united symbolically in a field that was enough of a cultural backwater to make me think I could take possession of it. In a life overdetermined by the need to unite a pair of parents who had never been together, my first serious effort was a curious amalgamation. Before arriving in New York I had put them together much more concretely in a piece of stunning and completely unconscious matchmaking. My old professor had returned with his wife to their home in Wellesley, and I was staying briefly in my old lady's house in Boston while she was ill in a hospital somewhere. One afternoon the professor came to see me at her house and we actually had intercourse in the bed in which her ancient, white-haired father stayed whenever he visited her. Welding the mythological parents together must have seemed imperative to strengthen my chances for survival in the real world. No support or encouragement would be forthcoming from my one natural parent. No other adult relatives were alive and available. My institutional life was over. I was on my own.

5

The Unknown Sex

Having left the institutions behind, I did my best to turn
New York into a facsimile of institutional life. I was still a
student, and I lived in rooms within apartments with common
kitchens and I related to the city as a school. The rest of the
city that was not a school was mysterious and terrifying:
everything that was not a school was the job market and the
streets. I entered the female slave market immediately as a
Christmas salesgirl selling stockings at Bonwit Teller. A regular saleswoman was furious when I sold a hundred boxes of
stockings over the counter to somebody; this didn't encourage
me to be a salesgirl. My next job was proofreading numbers
on endless big sheets of paper in an office where I could look
through a glass window and see several rows of women sitting
like tin soldierettes at typewriters on uniform gray, metal desks.
I had no idea what they were typing or what the numbers I
was proofreading represented or what the business was about.
After two weeks I walked away from the job. For eight months
I worked as a Schrafft's coffee girl on Thirteenth Street and
Fifth Avenue. I loved having breakfast there and leaving at
noon every day to attend my various classes. I loved browsing
after work in the Fourth Avenue bookstores and picking up
classics for a quarter. I did not love wearing my hair up under
a net, and I hated the subway I had to take to get there. The
subways objectified whatever it was about the city that trauma-
tized me—the noise, the crowds, the sheer size of the place,

the fact that there was more stone and concrete than sky, or that some people were in terrible shape and nobody else seemed to care, and that the whole environment seemed to be an asylum for sexual perverts. These were things I had never noticed when I was much younger and my mother took me shopping or to see a movie or a musical or for that matter to Schrafft's for lunch.

One morning on my way to work, as I approached the turnstile separating me from the steps to the street at the Fourteenth Street subway exit, I heard a sudden pounding of feet behind me and whirled around at the very moment my hips thrust forward involuntarily in reaction to being goosed. This particular pervert, and I was no stranger to them, shrank back into the shadows of the tunnel, regarding me over his shoulder with a maniacal look of defiance and glee. I recognized him as a wary dissolute character who had stared at me on previous mornings. One night I dreamt that a subway was powered by hundreds of bloody elephants' legs. Once I was on a subway that stopped in a tunnel between stations for an interminable period of time. The people sat embalmed in the silence and the flickering lights and the carbon dioxide effluence. I contracted a great subway phobia. Even long afterward I could be observed struggling desperately toward an exit in any crowded car. The slightest irregularity in the train's motion would cause me to flail through piles of bodies as if the scene were a mass suicide from which I was trying to escape. Eventually I discovered that I could get places without using the subways at all. I also learned to negotiate the streets like somebody whose city was occupied by guerrillas or foreign soldiers. In broad daylight, accompanied by friends, I was carefree enough; at night, even with friends, I developed eyes all over my body. The part of New York that was not a school was everything in passage, and whatever was in passage was fraught with danger.

This is not to say that New York was a bad place or even

that I thought it was. If anything, the problem with New York was me. I never perceived my new environment critically, as a place with a special character requiring particular adaptations. The way I survived in it was to react to it, like a rat in a laboratory experiment. I never anticipated problems that I might have avoided; I discovered problems by crashing into them. The idea that I was crashing into myself was very remote. I always felt victimized by circumstances, yet at the same time believed that everything was my own fault. In sum, nameless forces were treating me in the way that I deserved. This assumption was the basis for an old habit: doing things wrong to satisfy my understanding that I *was* wrong. In a design like that there were no problems, really, only wrongs (me) and rights (them). At that time, in any case, there was no atmosphere that might help one recognize problems undefined by the welfare agencies or charitable foundations; therefore in an important way such problems did not exist. The idea that living itself constitutes problems was unknown to me: either you were problem-free, or you had problems you were not supposed to have—both amounting to the same thing. The denial of problems was a staple of survival.

The essential problem as I see it was the denial of problems. I talked about myself as if I had problems, but all I was really saying was that I was bad, or inferior, and that I hoped people would like me nonetheless, or at least excuse me on the grounds that I was not responsible for what I was, and that they might even contradict me if they heard my complaints as pleas for love. Nobody I knew at that time complained about themselves the way I did; apparently I needed to feel that everybody else was good and strong and would therefore be able to take care of me if necessary. Behind "everybody else" stood my mother, whose own inadequacies were still obscure to me. I saw her as all-powerful and indomitable, regardless of certain images I had of her in passive, even abject, attitudes. I know she always fervently hoped the world would take care of me even if and/or because she failed to do so herself. I can imagine her holding her breath as I lurched through the jungle of New York—her provisions for me had never included exposure to the diversity and confusion of a big city. (Her own exposure to New York had been comfortably limited by the institutional setting of the Waldorf.) For several years in New York, I myself was not uncomfortably circumscribed by elements of a familiar background. Other people who were studying dancing were white, middle-class, college-educated Americans with modest ambition. The studio I attended every day was a professional extension of the college dance class. The work ethic and the self-improvement ethic were mutually understood in our daily exertions at the barre: devotion to art took precedence over material gain or security. Success at art meant being asked to join a company of one's choice. Courtesy and competition were coexistent ways of behaving. Personal difficulties were unacknowledged even to friends. Personal warmth was not the style in friendships—that is, expressions of caring were social rather than intimate or physical. The lives we led were those of very active people who were emotionally sedated and isolated, and in this milieu I did as well as I had in college or boarding school until it became apparent that dancing was not my destiny. Actually, however, in one fatal respect I was doing worse than before. I was no longer living exclusively with women, in whose company I had succeeded as a boy without being condemned as a girl. The opinions of men had not shaped my image of myself except through their impressions on my mother. Now, for the first time, I was exposed to contradictory opinions in an environment in which survival depended upon pleasing the unknown sex.

Dancing has always been a girl's profession par excellence, and American modern dance has been historically dominated by women, but I was studying with José Limón, a man who had just reached his prime as a leading dancer and choreographer. I went to him because of Doris Humphrey, whose prime had passed and who was at that moment his artistic director. Doris Humphrey was Martha Graham's contemporary and rival, but in her forties she succumbed to an arthritic hip, which turned her into a choreographer exclusively. American modern dance had been shaped by the concepts and techniques of these two women since the early thirties. In the fifties a student like me went to one or the other or to one of their great protégés. I was introduced to the Humphrey clan by my dance teacher in college. By nature I belonged to them. I would have been happy in an early Humphrey company of all women. One summer I danced in a revival of a twenties dance of hers for five women called *Soaring*. In the early days, companies and dances of women were very common. The women were all sizes, shapes, and looks, flouting the ballet and court traditions. José Limón was a Mexican-American who had danced with Humphrey and her partner, Charles Weidman, in the thirties. He was a big, magnificent-looking, Latin-Indian man who liked men. He was married to a woman who made his costumes and managed his career, but he was a lover of men nonetheless. The quality of his attention in class was a certain intimacy and camaraderie with the men. Any man who was big enough and fair looking merited special notice and the chance to join his company. A number of women fell by the wayside in this particular fraternity. The three women he already had in his company were rarefied editions of the pedestal type—one a dark, flashing, mature gypsy princess with temperament, the other two blond, soft, small, wholesome, delicate classics. Men and women were polarized masculine–feminine types; the soft men were absorbed in large group works. Had I really wanted to dance professionally, I would have gone to another studio. But since my ambitions were limited to excelling in the studio, I was in the right place. The possibility that another studio might have fired a greater ambition is a gratuitous question. The Limón classes suited my need to remain insulated from the world. Nothing in my background suggested a fantasy of public exposure. My one experience on the stage in Humphrey's *Soaring* was terrifying. Culture was still very intimidating. I was a student of culture, not a participant. In class also I could remain sexually undifferentiated. It was impossible to be either a boy or a girl in my newest surroundings. To compensate for not being a proper girl, I tried my best to be better than the boys. Thus I could go on being both in the torque of not being either. I imitated Limón's grand baroque style faithfully, arousing his pleasure and approval while confounding his sense of sexual place. He had no Amazons in his Olympic pantheon; he dominated his women completely. Later, when I became a critic, I paid him back. The way I escaped his studio without admitting defeat was by breaking a bone in my foot. In the meantime, suspecting defeat anyway, I took various steps to dissolve my unprofitable sexual neutrality.

To be correct, it was essential to feel one way and act another. Feeling and acting the same way is a privilege of only the ideally correct. Splitting love and sex is one of the more extraordinary human accomplishments. I already knew how to do it in several combinations. Apparently its purpose is to preserve certain feelings that sex is unable to accommodate. Feelings are easier to hide or distort than any activity they are meant to support. In my life in New York I preserved two sets of feelings: one for my own sex and the other for the old man who represented my father. On behalf of both, I was secretly in love with one of Limón's three women while occasionally sleeping with some man. I would not equate the two kinds of feelings: that for my own sex was the one integrated with erotic interest; that for the old man attached to some idea of wisdom and perfection. By sleeping with strange men I approached normalcy and protected my displacement. But to be truly correct it was essential to unite feeling and action, at least to the extent of successfully fooling myself, and to that end I arranged a miserable scene illustrating the folly of my double life and ritualizing the end of it—for the time being. Then I extracted a confession from my mother that set the stage for my first dangerous enterprise: marriage.

Two kinds of marriages transpired in the space of a couple of years as my old life dissolved in a shambles of embarrassing incidents. One was a conventional legal marriage and the other a mythic reordering of the two figures who had delivered me to the life I was then leading. The figure in New York who replaced my Boston dance teacher was a beautiful dancer in the Limón company. She was much younger, and fairer, and she was distracted by an affair with a violinist, but she represented success in dancing in the larger world, and she was interested enough in me to fuel a fantasy of obtaining her. Whether I obtained her or not was of no consequence next to the importance of the fantasy, which got me through four years of struggling at the barre. Limón himself was never a candidate for my mythological needs, nor were any other men associated with dance. Limón was certainly impressive, and I loved imitating him and being one of his "children"—but male dancers, much less Mexican-Indian ones, did not approximate my father archetype. The male I was closest to was Chester, an exquisite boy in Limón's company who lived with another boy—it was impossible to be friends with the boys who liked girls without being considered quarry. There may have been some special way of being friends with them, but I never learned what it was. I tried to relate to them intellectually, which was all wrong and very discouraging. My female friends were not intellectual, nor was the boy who was my close friend and who lived with another boy. I did make friends with one boy in class who was intellectual and ambitious and sexually ambivalent or at least sexually safe, but our friendship was not reciprocal because I always deferred to him by letting him regale me with his own ideas. Then, alas, he turned into a white knight when I fell victim to a sleazy episode involving a mutual acquaintance.

This mutual acquaintance was the best man I could find to fill out the male half of my parental archetype in New York. Time was running out, perhaps, and I had to hurry to complete the pair in order to meet the requirements of a new cycle. Anyway, my intellectual male dancer friend, Michael, was also a student at Columbia where I was studying, and through him I met several friends of his who were all good-looking, intense, exceptional Jewish boys like Michael. One of them seemed older, perhaps because he had a mustache and was a bit portly, and he was not so much attending the university as hanging around it. The others called him a hanger-on. Later they called him a pathological liar. His name was Lothar, a good name for a villain, and he played a good villain part. I have no visceral memory of why I liked him. I can imagine that I was impressed by the way he pictured himself as a poet and world traveler, but he was definitely a sleaze. His purpose in my life just then was, as it seems now, to be the agent of a great commotion that would make everybody think I was normal. The commotion functioned as a smoke screen behind which I organized a kind of primal scene detonating my whole life. Nothing in society offers a young man or woman immediate proof of gender/role identity so much as a pregnancy. Failing at dancing, as I thought I was, and failing to impress my idol enough to obtain her, and enjoying the friendship of two lovely girls whose primary interest was boys, and hanging around with boys whose interest in each other was much stronger than any interest they had in me, I went to bed with Lothar and immediately became pregnant. And since Lothar was a bastard and I had no resources, my various friends formed a kind of rescue mission of which I was the besieged star. Clearly if dancing was not a medium of recognition, being a woman was. A fear of recognition was no doubt the real motive in this sudden demonstration of my sex. A fear of

ABOVE: MY MOTHER WITH HER FATHER IN HUNTINGTON, LONG ISLAND, 1910.

LEFT: MY MOTHER WITH HER FATHER AND MOTHER — A "FATHER'S DAUGHTER."

BELOW: MY MOTHER (SEATED ON GROUND) WITH HER MOTHER, AUNTS, UNCLES, AND COUSINS — THE BAKER'S FAMILY IN AMERICA.

A BIG CHANGE IN MOTHER AT
EIGHTEEN — EXTROVERTED
AND ATHLETIC.

BELOW: WITH HER FAVORITE
COUSIN, HARRY, WHO
COMMITTED SUICIDE.

LEFT: MY COUSIN EDDIE, ON VACATION AT
ASBURY PARK AND (BELOW LEFT) WITH MY
MOTHER, ABOUT 1920. A "DANDY" AND A
LITTLE GUY.

ABOVE: MY MOTHER IN VENICE, 1925.

ABOVE LEFT: MY MOTHER AND I AT LONG BEACH FLANKED BY COUSINS NORMA AND ARLENE. ABOVE RIGHT: THE SAME AGE AT EDDIE'S HOUSE IN GREAT NECK. RIGHT: WITH A "GREAT WHITE FATHER" AT LAKE PLACID, AGE FOUR. BELOW: IN MY GRANDMOTHER'S HOUSE IN LITTLE NECK, AGE EIGHT.

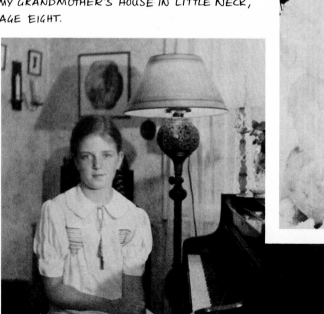

TWENTY-SEVEN YEARS SEPARATE THESE GRADUATIONS: MY MOTHER'S (ABOVE) IN HUNTINGTON, 1919 OR 1920, AND MINE (BELOW), FROM ST. MARY'S IN PEEKSKILL, NEW YORK, 1947 — "NICE GIRLS," MINISTERS' DAUGHTERS, ETC.

LEFT: MY GRANDMOTHER, PAULINE CROWE, AT SIXTY.

RIGHT: MY MOTHER WITH HER FIRST-PRIZE OIL PAINTING AT A WALDORF-ASTORIA ART EXHIBITION, ABOUT 1940.

LEFT: MY YEARBOOK GRADUATION PORTRAIT FROM ST. MARY'S, 1947. THE FIRST AND LAST PERMANENT WAVE.

Above: My mother's favorite picture of herself at fifty-two, in 1951.

Left: My children, Winnie and Richard, 1962 or 1963, and (above left) with my mother in 1964.

ABOVE: (LEFT TO RIGHT) CHESTER WOLENSKI, MYSELF, JOSEPH GIFFORD, AND LORNA BURDSALL IN JOSEPH'S COMPANY, 1955 — A CONCERT AT THE YM-YWHA. BELOW: ROBERT RAUSCHENBERG AND ALEX HAY IN ONE OF ALEX'S DANCES AT JUDSON CHURCH, 1963. OPPOSITE: YVONNE RAINER (BELOW) AND MYSELF IMPROVISING TO BERLIOZ AT A WASHINGTON SQUARE ART GALLERY CONCERT, SUMMER 1964. PHOTOS BY PETER MOORE.

ABOVE: (LEFT TO RIGHT) LARRY RIVERS, ROBERT RAUSCHENBERG, GEORGE SEGAL, AND ROSLYN DREXLER (BY SEGAL), STOCKHOLM, 1974.

BELOW: JOHN CAGE WITH PLANT.

LEFT: MARK DI SUVERO

BELOW RIGHT: RICHARD
BELLAMY

BELOW LEFT: MERCE
CUNNINGHAM

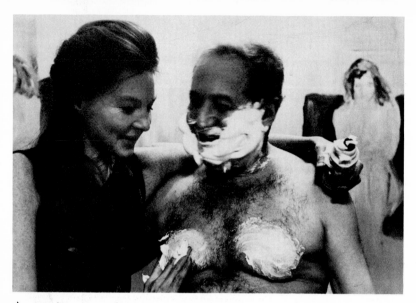

ABOVE: BARBARA FORST AND WALTER GUTMAN FOOLING AROUND IN THE SIXTIES.
BELOW LEFT: ALLEN GINSBERG READING AT A STOCKHAUSEN HAPPENING, 1964.
I'M SITTING AT HIS FEET, MOMENTARILY CHASTENED AND/OR CONTEMPLATING
MY NEXT MOVE IN MY ROLE AS "FREE AGENT." PHOTO BY FRED W. MCDARRAH.

ABOVE: SALLY GROSS AND HER
DAUGHTER, RACHEL, SAN FRAN-
SISCO, 1959.

ROBERT MORRIS AND YVONNE RAINER EMBRACING IN MORRIS'S "WATERMAN SWITCH," 1964.

LEFT: DARING LEAP FROM CHAIR INTO BOX — A "LECTURE-EVENT" AT BUFFALO ARTS FESTIVAL, 1965. BELOW: GEORGE SEGAL'S "DINNER TABLE" GROUP — I'M SEATED AT LEFT, WITH GEORGE, ALAN KAPROW, LUCAS SAMARAS ("ONE OF THE BOYS"); STANDING AT RIGHT IS ALAN'S WIFE, VAUGHAN RACHEL, AND, AT LEFT REAR, GEORGE'S HELEN. THE SCULPTURE RESIDES AT SCHWEBER ELECTRONICS ON LONG ISLAND.

ABOVE: HENRY
GELDZAHLER (AS BABE
RUTH), RED GROOMS,
AND MYSELF — A
"LECTURE-EVENT" AT
JUDSON CHURCH, 1963.
PHOTO BY PETER MOORE.

RIGHT: RAINER AND
FRIENDS IN GROUP WORK
WITH MATTRESSES, 1963.

ONE SORT OF SIXTIES LOOK — CONSPICUOUS, AND AVARICIOUS FOR A GOOD TIME. PHOTO BY FRED W. MC DARRAH.

failure lay behind that fear. If I succeeded (in dance) at all, I could just as easily fail at it, and I would certainly not want to fail in a medium I was not that serious about. Or I would want to forestall that possibility by some personal diversion. Just then I was rehearsing with a small company for a concert at the 92nd Street YM-YWHA—a proving ground for many dancers and choreographers. An abortion could dramatize my inner (unacknowledged) plan to terminate my brief life as a dancer. Surely it isn't really a fetus that one aborts. The sacrifice of an unborn child seems too unfortunate to be an end in itself. The whole event is too distressing to be considered anything other than a message in code—a code that may never be understood, although the event can be disturbing enough to cause a major realignment of direction. Obviously that must have been what I had in mind, since my life would soon be dramatically different.

I had two sets of friends representing the two interests I was pursuing independently of each other. These friends and interests were the gifts of my philosophy professor and my dance teacher. Four years had passed since I had had sex with my professor in Boston in the apartment of my dance teacher. Now, in an apartment in New York belonging to another mentor, I gave birth to a fetus that could plausibly be traced to the old man. Lothar had long shipped out around the world on the Isthmian line. My dancer friend was on tour or rehearsing in a studio someplace in the city. I had somehow managed to arrange another scene welding together my mythological pair. In this renewed attempt to locate the pair inside me, I destroyed "their" child. The blood was terrible, and I thought I was hemorrhaging to death, so I called the police, who brought a stretcher and an ambulance and drove me to Roosevelt Hospital—by coincidence, the hospital where my mother had once trained as a nurse. There my two sets of friends arrived to view the remains, or the beginnings, and my drama was complete. That year I wrapped it all up as a dancer and became a serious intellectual dance critic. But since a career of any kind was still intimidating, I contrived to hide behind the most acceptable identity for a woman and got married. Protecting myself from a career, however, was hardly reason enough, by itself anyway, to get married.

It was only my mother's unwilling cooperation that made this possible. The best reason to get married was finding out that my mother never had. The faithful imitation of parents is often accomplished best by reaction; by actually doing what they didn't do or vice versa, we're doing what they wished they might have done had they been able to. In some cases that means just continuing their work where they left off. My mother's failure to marry eclipsed much of her feeling of well-being—the necessity of posing as a widow and concealing or twisting her real story eclipsed much of her social life. Since marriage was not as meaningful in my own time as in hers, marrying to remedy her loss was more urgent than marrying to make myself feel better than she ever did. The gesture itself meant more than any commitment to it. I could imitate my mother's attitude no matter what I did that was different; then, if it didn't work out, I could imitate her completely. Marriage was the leitmotif of my mother's story; concealment of her marriage status was central to the story—her security depended on it, and any threat to this security aroused her wrath and terror. My own security depended completely upon hers, but I had no idea what would threaten it. I found out as soon as I confronted her with the truth, which she was unable to deny and equally unable to come to terms with. Actually I only suspected the truth and then asked her to confirm it. I had never been interested in her "marriage" one way or the other until this moment. It had been five years since she sent me the news of my father's death when I was in college, and then the news of his death had interested me much more than my mother's accompanying letter explaining that she was no longer a widow but a divorcée. I never paused to consider why she had said she was a widow in the first place. The logic of her moves was lost in my excitement over the man who suddenly had at least one extra life; I must have filed her new story in a mental drawer marked "to be investigated later."

I had little to do with my mother in the next five years. I was busy studying and was preoccupied with my love affairs, and my meetings with her were not encouraging. Then, as I passed into the critical transition period marking the end of my various preparations to do something in the world, I pressed her into service. The key to her new role in my life was her story, which had evidently sorted itself out in the drawer where it was filed. To make it available, all I had to do was bang into it somehow. As it happened I banged into it at the movies. I was watching *East of Eden* starring James Dean—it must have been 1955 or '56—when the startling idea formed in my consciousness that my mother had never been married. Apparently the association was provided by Dean's discovery of his mother, whom his father had always said was dead, and further, the revelation that she was a whore. I was now well into my twenties and about to discover something critical about my mother and our relationship—that something out there, society or whatever it was, was more important to my mother than our relationship or even than she was to herself. Between us, like a giant wall, stood an abstraction called marriage. But this had not always been the case— when I was little, she had been able to enjoy me without fear of exposure. Now I knew her dread secret, and she felt guilty enough to imagine that there was no reason why I would stand in protection of her. In short, my mother was very angry. I have a dim recollection of confronting her north of New York somewhere, standing near a pond, or in a parking lot, or outside a building—probably near the place where she was working then: a psychiatric hospital for rich people. Then I know we got into her car to drive off somewhere, but I recall only two details from the whole scene. I hurled the coffee I was carrying in a paper cup at the car door; and each of us accused the other of being what all along she was afraid we really were: I called her a whore and she called me a bastard. *East of Eden* had been like a sneak preview of this movie with my mother. It was the first open lesion between us. I had never done anything worse than lose things or spill them or ignore her; I had failed to appreciate her, certainly, but I never had anything on her. In a flash our positions shifted drastically, and a tacit agreement was reached to realign our mutual protection racket, since neither of us could afford a total breakdown in our relationship. If I had in the past deserved her protection as the unwitting issue of her misadventure, I now had to *win* her protection by some gesture of good faith. I was not mature or knowledgeable enough to condone her actions or forgive her outbursts, but I was fearful and clever enough to devise a move that would appease her and reestablish a buffer zone between us. The buffer of my (lost) ignorance had to be replaced by a kind of smoke screen for my sudden intelligence. My mother's protection had always wavered whenever she perceived me at odds with the forces that had molded her own acts and attitudes—her instinct at those moments was always to turn me in. It was after all only her belief in the system she had defied that made our situation what it was. Her wavering protection, in turn, was the chink in her own armor—that is, in her determination to maintain her secret. The less she protected me, the greater the likelihood I would discover her vulnerability. Now her secret was out and my protection was gone, and no special insight was required to see that a marriage could set us right for the time being. By demonstrating a shared belief in the system that threatened us both, I could put some distance between us without making things worse. Our efforts, then, to survive each other as well as society included my marriage. All this may sound as if I knew exactly what I was doing, but of course I didn't, and I only got married when it appeared to be my last or sole choice. I was still a perfectly unconscious young girl, and I only did things in reaction to other things that had proved untenable. As old arrangements dissolved, I set up new ones the way pebbles rearrange themselves on a beach with every wave. Now a big rearrangement was about to take place —a career and a marriage—and the beach site I picked out was the New York Public Library on 42nd Street, the great building in the center of it all, guarded by two granite lions. Here once more I welded together my mythological parents, but this time I united them in a career and married the symbolic male.

The moment I stopped dancing I went to the library to apply for a job, or perhaps I stopped dancing as soon as I took the job and began working. I was hired by Genevieve Oswald, the curator of the Dance Collection, who had obtained a Rockefeller grant to hire help in sorting out clippings and cataloguing photographs. My new dancing lady was a librarian. My "intellectual man" appeared eventually in the cafeteria. But I was surrounded by him in all his books and dissertations. One day in the form of an old man with white hair he walked into the Dance Collection and asked me if I wanted to write some dance reviews. This old man was Louis Horst, a venerable dance world figure who published a distinguished but little-known trade rag called the *Dance Observer*. Once upon a time he was Martha Graham's lover, composer, and mentor, and one summer I had studied choreography with him at Connecticut College. That year I had submitted to his publication the first thing I ever wrote besides letters and school essays, and the sight of my name in print at the top of the article when it appeared catalyzed my interest in criticism and writing. I had barely begun, and my ambition was extensive; already I fancied myself America's leading dance critic. I imagined, I think, inheriting the mantle of several dead or retired old men. (I was collecting such old men.) I especially

admired a German critic called Artur Michel who died in
America right after the war, and I was in awe of John Martin,
who was about to retire from the *New York Times*. I shared
the opinion of many dancers that Edwin Denby, who wrote
for the *Tribune* during the war, was the most sensitive and
poetic critic of the ballet. I discounted Walter Terry (the
critic Denby had replaced for that time), who was active and
middle-aged. (Although John Martin was only retiring, I
developed the idea somehow that he had died. A woman who
sometimes substituted for Martin and who came into the
library a lot was also preparing dance obituaries for the *Times*.
Somehow I equated Martin's retirement with death, possibly
because I secretly wanted his job and thought the best way to
get it was to kill him off—a more definitive ending, after all,
than mere retirement—and/or because my history as the
daughter of a "dead man" had prepared me for such extreme
deeds. Twenty years later I found out that Martin was very
old but alive and well in northern New York State someplace.)
During the ten months I worked at the library I also had the
opportunity to see a dead man for the first time. That year
Arturo Toscanini died, and I went to see him laid out at the
Frank Campbell funeral parlor because his son Walter was a
friend of my boss, Genevieve Oswald. I was very curious and
personally unaffected. I can't remember whether the thought
of my own dead father crossed my mind or not—it may have,
but in general he wasn't on my mind, or if he was, he was
sublimated completely in my cultural investigations.

I was still deeply immersed in culture without locating
myself in it; while I went merrily on about culture, my personal
life conducted itself on its own as if on automatic pilot—I
paid no attention to it except when I crashed into it. My life
was not a frame of reference like art or dance history or the new
French novel. It was not even a biography like any biography
I had ever read. If it was anything, it was something to avoid
or ignore for fear that it wasn't right. The terrible incident with

my mother, for instance, was enough to make me redouble my attention to culture. The most exciting thing I did at the library was to stay on after hours translating a book, published in 1911, about the court ballet in France before Louis XIV.

But while I was learning about the court ballet and sorting clippings and cataloguing photos, a drama was developing between me and my boss. My boss, who was an exuberant attractive woman in her thirties, was dedicated to her Dance Collection while I was not—I was there in my own behalf and she thought I was there in hers. I did my job, but my attitude as a helper was that I had better things to do. I was excited about the collection but not for its own sake or for its public utility. I acted really as if I were the public myself—there to be serviced by the collection and its enthusiastic curator. The curator no doubt sensed this and made efforts to put me in my place. Very often I felt as if I was minding the store while she attended to the more glamorous aspects of her business. She breezed in late and talked to important people and went to fancy lunches and told me what to do and left early for home, whereas I had to punch the clock and look busy filing all the time and wear my hair in a bun and pretend that my job was a privilege. Eventually, anyway, I became enormously hostile, and since I had no apparent cause to be, and had I been aware of one, wouldn't have thought it justified, I acted like a child in the same circumstances—withdrawn and sullen and sometimes inexplicably demonstrative. I would move boxes around with undue clatter, and at length I stopped speaking altogether as if I were on strike. I had learned how to do this very well from my mother—whenever she was seriously displeased with me she went on strike in this manner, clamming up for hours or even days, refusing to speak until I repented or she relented or the world around us changed us somehow. The two of us would keep company in painful silence like this for hours or even days on end. At the library I treated my boss as if she were my mother; she was the first woman who intimidated me and displeased me the way my mother did. I hadn't given any other woman this kind of power over me without a romantic commitment, and the kinds of romances I had had to date weren't defined by the power struggles obtaining between me and my mother—I had never opposed their interests or threatened to exceed or diminish them. The power of my boss was untempered by romance or friendly interest or motherly concern. Her romance was with her collection and not me; mine was with my unfolding ambition, which had nothing to do with her. Mainly it had nothing (or everything) to do with my mother, the social guardian of a daughter's place. The mother who opposes a daughter's ambition just at its unfolding can be found any- and everywhere. Ambitions that were never nurtured or encouraged are generally implemented through opposition. My boss at the library was a convenient and proper antagonist. As I set myself against her, she endured until springtime and then, quite naturally, simply fired me.

As a result, I was thrown up against my mother, who found no reason to champion me against another mother; instead, she sent me to a shrink who suggested I had a problem with my mother. This was outstanding news to me. At last I had something personal to ponder. At last somebody had *said* something about my personal life. At last I had a personal life. Not even the terrible confrontation with my mother over her "marriage" had made me think I had a problem or that anything was wrong. A whole new era was about to begin. I had a problem with my mother! I could see my mother in a certain light—she was a problem! And that was the extent of her new definition. The possibility of a solution had not been broached. The only solutions I considered were unilateral and exclusive. The most obvious solution was an ally—I had never had an ally against my mother. As my war with the curator at the library escalated, an ally put in an appearance. This was my "intellectual man"—the counterpart to my dancing lady, who had turned into a rival and opponent. Surely at this moment only an intellectual man was a suitable ally in a daughter's war against her mother. Practically the moment I left the library I was married.

I wasn't through with my mother so easily, however. As summer was approaching and I was suspended between lives, she tried to reclaim our childhood together on her island retreat in Maine. There I joined her and waited proverbially, as on "foreign shores," for the young man who wanted me to marry him to come and take me away.

6

Abandoned
in Marriage

The young man who wanted me to marry him was a mere boy of twenty-one who was already married. He was handsome and clean-cut and six years younger than me—he could have been a younger impossible brother. Our relationship was at once companionable and murderous. As I was, in a sense, my mother's younger impossible sister, I found in him a variant of the relationship I knew best. But if the murderous aspect of my relationship with my mother had always been latent, it now became the order of the day in my life with a boy; by this tactic I avoided its becoming the order of the day with my mother. More important, a total rupture with her was averted. By shifting the arena of conflict just when it threatened to become overt, we preserved the semblance of harmony required to hold things together. At her summer retreat in Maine, the shift occurred like a kind of changing of the guard. Swan's Island was still nearly as remote and safe from tourism as it had been when my mother took me there as a child. The ferry from Bass Harbor was still a fishing boat, and the summer folk were house owners and their friends or relatives. My mother had gone there originally with her friend Bertha Hatch, who owned a sweet old house nestled on a rocky cliff facing the sunset. I remembered seals in the cove below and my mother swimming in the icy water and photos of myself clambering on the rocks. Now Bertha was not there, her house was boarded up, and my mother had rented a rambling white house near the water on another part of the island.

We had not spent "real" time together in years; possibly my mother harbored a notion that if we started all over again, things would go differently and for the better. But I was very hostile and I had lots of books with me that I deemed superior to her company. And I intended to leave her soon for a strange boy. A belated teen-age rebellion was the essence of this experimental trip together. On the one hand, she resented my dependency, and on the other, she was enraged by the threatened loss of it. And I felt the same way. I hadn't actually lived with her since I was a small child. Thus, we were more attached and dependent than many mothers and children who break away at more conventional times. Nobody would have said we were close, but our very distance bespoke a bond that had never been cut. Our vacation together in Maine was a token of the life we had never led since I was five, and it provided a pretext for rebellion and separation. The island itself was a perfect setting—it made us more alone together and set our conflict in high relief. Then, when I left her there, I left as if abandoning a shipwreck; she was beached, as it were, and I was picked up by a passing schooner. The passing schooner was the strange boy I intended to marry who arrived one day on the island ferry carrying a battered black suitcase. The island could have been England to which my mother and I had returned to conceive a "real boy." I did indeed conceive (a son) there, and without a doubt we did it together, with the assistance of the "passing schooner." Anyway, the main issue was our struggle, of which we relieved ourselves through the birth of a third party. The only noteworthy incident before the "schooner" arrived was very telling: in a fit one afternoon, I dropped two raw eggs at my mother's feet. Food best symbolized our dependency problems: she resented making it and serving it, and I paid her back with my carelessness. Serving was equivalent to spending, and whatever she spent on me seemed to be for a lost cause; there was no return of appreciation, in other words. And now I was giving myself away to a boy, and the boy I described to her seemed like another lost cause, inasmuch as he was already married. To me, however, that was the least of the problems he presented.

That he was married in fact might actually have recommended him to me. Not because a fear of marriage made his marriage a reassuring obstacle, though that may have been in my mind, but because the way he had gotten married suited a need I had to reconstruct my mother's story. Like my father, he was not inclined to marry his girl friend just because she was pregnant, but unlike my father, his parents wanted the baby and pressured him to marry her. He had an old-fashioned shotgun wedding, at the rather traditional age for those things of nineteen. His young wife bore a son and he left home alone for New York, leaving himself behind, as it were, in security or in escrow. Now he wanted a divorce in order to advance himself in this manner again perhaps. If I went along with the model I could be left alone with a child the way my mother had been, but the child would be legitimate and so finally would I. The key to my suitor's story was his marriage under pressure. I was not the least bit enlightened about marriage. Not having been slated for marriage, yet gathering the impression from my mother's paroxysm over it that it was tremendously important, it would naturally be something I would do under pressure and not by any considered choice. The utmost convention was at work in my own story: the only reason to marry was to be legitimate. Nothing in my mother's life or words suggested men as desirable partners; nothing in my own life to date suggested them as that either. Yet I had to imagine them, or at least one of them, that way in order to enter into marriage—it was simply inconceivable to marry solely for the sake of legitimacy. Nonetheless, by aligning myself with a boy who required a divorce to make our son legitimate, that was what I was doing. The trick was to summon up the feelings that would warrant such a finality as marriage. The real pressure was on my feelings, which balked at an object that would clearly make me proper rather than happy. It was not my fate to be both proper and happy, but the effort to be proper was only possible in tandem with at least an illusion of happiness. And since propriety is invested with happiness, I attached my feelings to that social reality. I commenced once again to be in love with love, or with the propriety of the object.

The difference this time was that I had to live with it. There was no protection from being with him, no time or distance between the idea and the reality of him. The idea of him groaned with reality from the start—the engagement was inescapable. It seemed as if our very first meeting had been prearranged: he saw me in the cafeteria of the library and asked me out right away, and after we went out, we went to bed, and after we went to bed, he thought we should get married. The thought of not getting married never occurred to me—he was too good looking and serious and intellectual and ambitious, and his approach to making love to girls was to satisfy them. His approach to satisfying himself was not so appealing; he would close his eyes in the missionary position and work on it by himself for a long, harrowing period of time, and his attitude to sex was that he needed it daily. But these ominous signs were not apparent enough to affect my rash commitment to the future. Or they were and they signified a certain determination on his part that assured me of his genuine interest. He was very serious and determined, which both reassured me and frightened me. His life situation was as critical as mine was, and the custom then was to act things out or internalize them rather than make them conscious. He readily found girls available to relieve himself with, and I was a typically repressed unconscious girl. Making myself available to a young disturbed boy was my first sustained personal exposure. I had to begin to act things out myself or I would implode from being acted upon. In the meantime, I was simply suspended with fear, which I expressed in the manner of one who has nowhere to go. I was leaving for Maine soon, but I was joining my mother, who now seemed dangerous to me. And I had agreed to being pursued there by a boy I really hardly knew. Before leaving I spent four days with him virtually sunk in nausea. Anticipating the future, I expressed a wish to halt it or drive it away with this severe attack of nausea. It could be said that I was making a final approach to normalcy through storms of objections from my internal displacement bureau. The urgent wish to be elsewhere was simulated by nausea. In Maine several weeks later, when Schooner arrived with his battered black suitcase, I was intensely nauseated again for about forty-eight hours. My relief at seeing him was quickly overcast by my fear of him.

I now had protection from my mother and no protection from my protector. A friend of my mother's defined marriage as a state of "two against the world"; I hadn't had such an ally since I had my mother when I was small. As ally and protector, my mother's worst fault was maintaining me in ignorance; that is, I was overprotected. This is not a bad preparation for marriage, insofar as girls have traditionally been passed in ignorance from family to husband; however I was even more ignorant than a traditionally ignorant girl. The one thing even an ignorant girl knows is her place in relation to boys, and in this respect I was not prepared for marriage at all. Under my mother's protection, I had never learned my place as a girl; I was ignorant but not submissive, a combination guaranteed to doom any marriage. I was marrying to be legitimate, but I had acquired the psychology of the illegitimate, or I should say I was born that way. Born in defiance of marriage, in submission only to my mother's will, and raised apart from those who might have judged her (and reformed or redeemed me), I could only marry to defy my mother—a gesture that could leave me stranded between her and men. As an ally, my young husband gave me support that lasted as long as his pleasure did; from one point of view, that equaled the duration of the marriage, which was four years. While we remained married and lived together he could always hold out for his pleasure. Much as I might have wanted to be a regular sort of girl who accepts sex for the sake of marriage, I quickly disqualified myself in that capacity. I enjoyed sex myself, but was repelled by the exertions of my partner on his own behalf. In any case, no sooner was I pregnant than I succumbed to an infection common in pregnancies that made sex impossible. To assert that my Schooner's security or sense of himself was inseparable from his pleasure would be asserting the least of it. He was utterly young and unaccomplished in any other way. He had come up from the Midwest to finish college in New York and attach himself somehow to the Eastern Establishment. His parents were discouraged working middle-class people who had invested their only son (and child) with as much fear as hope. His strategy for survival and advancement early centered around his conquest of girls—he stoked and gauged his ambition by the limits of his sexual success. His assessment of me as a proper object was reasonably misguided, nor was mine of him any more intelligent. But we were just as suitable to each other as we were not. My resistance and his obduracy gave each of us the excuse finally to move on. And our struggle while it lasted didn't impair the image we created of a proper couple.

My refusal or inability to submit was itself endemic to my position; it certainly wasn't a lack of desire or effort to succeed that made me fail. I frequently forced myself to do things I hated doing in order to appear successful; in particular I did these things when I felt most strongly that I was failing. I ironed his shirts once, I remember, in a fit of remorse (and fear) over my incompetence. Once when I was seven or eight months pregnant, I helped him get off in a manner so disgusting to me that I nearly lost control over the laughter I had to suppress. I had good reason to do my best sexually in every way because he felt exceedingly insecure when I was unavailable—no excuse was guarantee against his violence when I was unable to have sex. The moment I was pregnant and infected, I was a sexual failure. We had left my mother and the island and taken a bus to Boston where we rented a room for two weeks. Schooner took a job in a laundromat and I brought him his lunch every day. One day I had to stop in every dark secluded doorway to relieve the unbearable itching of my infectious discharge. By the time I reached a hospital for help, I had torn my membrane apart, or rendered it so raw and inflamed that in order to pee it was necessary to coat the area with a heavy white ointment called Desitin—so much for enjoying sex. The infection was so virulent and tenacious, a strain especially attached to pregnancy, that throughout the rest of my term it would recur in force the moment I thought it was safe to indulge my desire and/or satisfy my eager partner. My partner found this obstacle to his gratification extremely inconvenient, to say the least, and fortunately for me he was called away by the army for a few months and not released until my term was approaching its end and I had a better excuse to deprive him than when I was merely infected. His attitude toward my infection was that I had it on purpose to torment him, and indeed perhaps I did have it on purpose— not to torment him, though, but to evade him. I was terribly sorry about tormenting him because it compounded my discomfort. I could certainly see or sense what a vicious circle the whole thing was. Each evasion evoked new and more ingenious evasions in response to his escalated attacks. The marriage was like an army in retreat pursued to the bitter end by a determined loser. Who was truly the loser it would be difficult to say. I retreated and he pursued and occasionally I would take a stand and lash out absurdly, thus endangering my life. Surely I was the loser in any conventional sense: he was stronger and more intimidating, and I tended to feel guilty while he always felt justified, and in the end he walked away leaving me holding two little kids.

By then practically everything he did was abhorrent to me, but I wanted at all costs to remain married. Yet I colluded effectively in ending it. I think my fear of not surviving within the marriage was greater than my fear of what might happen when it was over. I had married to be proper, not to be happy, but if I grew too unhappy I could be proper and dead. I could at least have pretended I was happy if I had felt more secure—the investment of propriety with happiness surely depends on security—but I was so insecure that my pretense at happiness was intermittent and short-lived. Then all that counted was looking proper, and behind that façade I could easily die, especially since the more insecure I felt, the more tightly I clung to the marriage, and the more I did that, the worse things got. But the worse things got, the closer the end was. We were living in a ground-floor railroad apartment in Washington Heights. I was teaching at a private girl's school and writing for a magazine and a newspaper and pushing a baby carriage to the park every day. I can't remember if I was still trying to cook and iron shirts or not, but I had long become sexually remote. Schooner was working nine-to-five jobs as a clerk and going to school at night, and his answer to sexual frustration was to find a girl friend at school. My sense of insecurity reached a new nadir, and my response was helplessness and inaction: any constructive move on my part could prolong the marriage. I wouldn't have known what to do in any case, short of the one thing I was by then incapable of doing, but the best way to end the marriage was to imagine I still wanted it. It wasn't difficult imagining I wanted a social commodity with such a high premium on it. Anyway, by imagining I still wanted it, I felt tormented enough to justify its conclusion. Naturally I felt tormented wanting something I was losing—especially something I was losing through my own fault. Loss itself is a condition of prizing something; a sense of failure always attends a loss. As soon as I wanted the marriage I no longer had it—I wouldn't have wanted something I already had. When I felt I was losing it, I wanted it; then the more I wanted it, the faster it went. And, of course, the faster it went, the worse I felt, as events confirmed my failure.

Typically, I appealed outside the marriage for help. Appeals of this nature are really complaints, which are best answered by agreement. The help I got was the unpleasant reflection of my own opinion. Certain anonymous help probably saved my life. I had one creative habit of bolting for the door whenever violence portended or erupted. I had the best chance at this when I provoked an attack myself, as when I threw Schooner's T. S. Eliot poems out the window and he chased me through the door and down the street with a toilet plunger. My pride, should I have had any, was eclipsed by the need for witnesses. On that occasion I attracted a small crowd by the commotion I created dodging my assailant and yelling in flight. I had not always been so demonstrative. Like my mother, I never yelled or cried or threw things or hit anybody—instead of yelling or crying for help, I would find some reason to go to the hospital. I never believed I needed help: that would amount to defeat, and then other people would think I needed help, and obviously I would stay that way. The best way to get help was to appeal to the helping agencies that respond to acceptable problems. Being abandoned in a marriage was never an acceptable or understood problem; I refused to accept it myself, and at some point lodged the complaint in my chest. The way it got there,

I surmise, was by swallowing yells (of pain and rage). Eventually all these yells imploded in my chest and caused me to suffocate. The site of this dramatic event was mid-Manhattan one evening at the ballet. I was sitting in the balcony with Schooner and some students watching a Balanchine ballet when my chest detonated with pain, taking my breath away. Schooner removed me to the hospital, where they said I had viral pneumonia and kept me a week. That was a big help. The only other time I got away was when I flew to Cuba to see if we could abort my daughter. First we tried to convince some medical authorities in New York that another baby would be hazardous to my health. Failing that, I contacted a dancer friend married to a Cuban revolutionary who was commandant of the Oriente province. My friend encouraged me to fly there but was unable to obtain an abortionist when I arrived. I enjoyed the trip but on returning had to contend with Schooner, who was furious over spending three hundred dollars for nothing. I had a better excuse to get away when my mother asked me to join her in Maine for a week. However my mother was no help. By then she was happy I was married and would be terrified if I told her what was really happening. Appealing to my mother for help was like seeking a death warrant for the marriage.

In this my mother was ever a true helper, reflecting and magnifying my own worst opinion of things. Her approach to life in general was that either everything was wonderful or all was lost. If all seemed lost, she was ready to close the case, and my case would now soon be closed. My mother by this time considered herself a grandmother, and I was free to be something besides her daughter. The purpose of the marriage had been fulfilled: between us stood two new relatives who were promising receptacles for her attention. Of the two, naturally, it was my daughter she really prized. At this moment in her life, my mother was recovering from her last affair. As if my daughter were her own, she had arranged to be in love with a man who would disappoint her the way my father had. My marriage and her affair covered approximately the same period of time, and as my marriage foundered and her affair ended, another girl was born over the "grave" of a man. Or in this case two men. Like my mother's mother, I was properly married but just as subversive. Having discharged an inherited task of advancing a female line, I too was pressed to dispose of the agency of birth. My grandmother was widowed young, having herself been orphaned at eight, my mother was a widow by fraud, and I would be separated and divorced.

The doubtful project of a female line remained an unexplored issue. My mother had enjoyed herself as a child, and she lamented the end of my own childhood. Now she would enjoy herself as a child in my daughter and lament the end of my daughter's childhood as well. The reflection of a mother in her daughter as a child seemed to be the sole purpose of a female line.

Not only had I needed a daughter to appease my mother, but I needed an intellectual husband to reflect my own interests. The boy I married was young and angry and very intellectual—he wanted to be a poet, a literary critic, and a banker like T. S. Eliot. His attitude toward me as an intellectual was self-serving and superior: my two degrees were tokens of esteem but not guarantees or indications of authority. His superiority was invaluable in one respect and simply irritating in another. In the latter regard we never exchanged ideas; we fought over them. In the former, he acted like a tutor in the matter of my writing; he was my first editor and counselor. Apparently the need of his ego was greater than his fear of not being served by a proper wife, or perhaps he thought he could advance my interests and have a proper wife as well, and/or that he would be rewarded by my appreciation, thereby justifying his encouragement. But I was never really a proper wife, and nothing he did or didn't do was going to make me one. I only wanted to *appear* proper in order to front my ambition, in which I had no confidence. The end of the marriage was a disaster from this point of view. Being free to be something besides my mother's daughter did not mean being on my own. If I was no longer a daughter or a wife, I was not yet established as a critic, and I had no resources, emotional or financial, for carrying on alone with two children. Therefore I flailed about for a period of time trying to save myself. The next phase of my life represented a struggle to be my mother's daughter—the daughter she had loved as a child—in the world at large. A new mentor was essential—the father principle in some guise— and a new mother who thought I was wonderful. And so once again I located or invented my dancing lady and her mythical companion—the man of culture and intellect.

7

A Wild Party

Now I was older and my mentors were getting younger, but I reverted to my earliest emotional model in the choice of sex. I never again found a man emotionally satisfying, or I should say fancied one that way, and the women I found were as ambivalent as my mother. The first woman I went to was a marriage counselor who warned me against women. I must have told her I had a hateful husband and I had once loved women, because she tried to convince me that a penis was better than a tongue. She was a very attractive, proper lady with white hair. Marriage counselors, after all, were not supposed to discourage marriage, but what I wanted to hear just then was that it was all right not to be married—in fact, that it could actually be for the best. And/or I needed a model of someone surviving in an unmarried or separated state. The woman I was closest to at that time was firmly married, and she and her husband, in particular her husband, took a dim view of the shambles of my marriage; but she introduced me to a friend of hers who suited my needs admirably. This friend, whose name was Sally, was a dancer and a mother and a wife whose marriage looked as bad as mine. She was also beautiful and exotic, by which I mean very different from me. She lived in the nether regions of Manhattan, an area south of Houston Street that I had never visited and knew nothing about. This was 1960, '61. The world was changing and some of us would be swept up in the change. A revulsion against being married and bourgeois made me susceptible to the changes taking place around me, or else the changing world was making it possible to entertain alternatives, thereby supporting my revulsion. I was still living in Washington Heights, and for a time I was reunited with my husband, but at heart I was living downtown.

The world downtown was a scene—its characters were artists, dancers, poets, art dealers, wives, mothers, mistresses, and hangers-on—and I had never been part of a scene. The dancers I knew in the fifties never made a scene; there were no parties or excursions or freakish events or masquerades. People in the fifties were sedate and grown-up. My new friend was leading a colorful life in a kind of apartment called a "pad" on the Lower East Side. Within a year, my own apartment would look very much like hers. When I was married, my mother had had my grandmother's antiques hauled out of storage and sent to me in Washington Heights. By the time I left Washington Heights, they were broken, lost, or abandoned. In fact it was over their loss and ruin that I left the Heights and moved downtown. I was not yet capable of making changes in my life consciously. For that matter I was not really aware of changes; I just went on moving or altering my circumstances in response to external pressures. I had no sense of control over events in which I appeared to be the protagonist. I never perceived myself as a protagonist. Anybody was a protagonist but me. In other words, I was still oriented to life as a child. I had two children who had the same power over me that the rest of the world did, or more, considering how close they were. I was at that point living alone with them in a fifth-floor walk-up several blocks from where we had lived with their father. I was no longer teaching, but I was writing for the same newspaper (the *Village Voice*) and the same magazine (*Art News*), and my social life was escalating wildly. My income from writing averaged eighty-five dollars a month. (The art magazine paid me; the newspaper was not yet solvent.) Sometimes my husband gave me twenty-five dollars a week.

For a few months I went on welfare, maintaining a phone and a car against welfare regulations. The car I maintained was a '55 Ford, which I parked on the street and used to cart my children with me everywhere in the city, door to door. By door to door I mean I parked as close as possible to mine and to those of my destinations, thus saving me one kind of trouble and incurring another in the form of innumerable parking tickets. I paid no more attention to these tickets than I did to the regulations by which I got them, so eventually I was summoned to court, where I was branded a scofflaw and fined lots of dollars in addition to the cost of the tickets. I had various improbable schemes for raising money besides my art magazine salary and welfare and intermittent alimony. One month to pay the rent I sold a George Segal pastel and another month a small Mark di Suvero sculpture. Once I convinced an art dealer to pay me in advance for an article I proposed to write about one of his artists. As an art critic, I qualified to accept or offer bribes in a common cause. The art dealer who advanced me money for the article also used his connections to make me a producer of dance concerts, for which I might receive enough to pay another month's rent. I no longer qualified for welfare after my case worker discovered I had a telephone.

In the summers my mother took my two children to the country in northwestern Connecticut, and I drove up every Sunday to see them. It was on one of these Sundays in July of 1963 that my life in Washington Heights came to an abrupt end. I was behind on my rent and had failed to take note of an eviction notice from the Marshall's office. Returning from Connecticut this particular Sunday in July '63, I found my apartment completely stripped and empty. The Marshall's men had removed many of my things to a storage depot downtown under the West Side Highway, and the rest, considered garbage, was strewn in the basement of the building in cans and burlap bags. I never recovered my baby album or my grandmother's Persian rug, perhaps my two most cherished possessions, and that same day I lost my wedding ring on the street, possibly dropping it under the car as I drove off hysterically in search of my new life. No less hysterically, of course, in mourning for my old one.

The upshot of all this was that I was left in one of my favorite positions—that of requiring help. The city had helped me already by second-guessing my next move, of which I was unaware myself. Even their storage depot was way downtown, where I had already been spending as much time as possible. City or state may be the last (or first) court of appeal in an undirected life. The move itself was largely implemented by my new friend Sally, who found an apartment on Houston Street and drove there with me to see it. The apartment was two floors over a tombstone business called Shastone Memorials and next to a garage and near a famous Jewish deli called Katz's and only a mile north of East Broadway where Sally lived. The rent was ninety dollars a month. At the end of the summer I retrieved my children from my mother in Connecticut and moved in. That year my husband obtained a divorce in Mexico and married a young woman who would play an important part in my life beginning in 1965, as stepmother to my children. From the fall of '63 until August '65 I was to lead the most intense and complex life it was possible to lead at that time, short of flying or traveling long distances. And this was what I was getting ready to do. The models of my past were now split in different capacities. Although the woman I admired was a dancer, it was not as a dancer that I admired her. And while the man who now influenced me the most was an intellect, he was primarily an artist.

My relationship to women at this point was shifting ground. As I was older and a critic, other women were trying to make a mentor out of me, a role I resisted and tried to deny. Although Sally was younger than me, she was definitely in command. She knew much more about life than I did, for she had been living her life while I had been studying some of life's artifacts. Comparatively, I really hadn't had a life at all, but had merely been enduring life as I immersed myself in the activities by which I abstracted myself from it. A dissolution of my personality was under way at this time: My life-support system just wasn't adequate to bear the weight of all my distractions. Financially and emotionally my situation was constantly tenuous. Ignoring practical matters to pursue emotional satisfaction, I remained out of touch with my emotions excepting heroic or romantic ones. My self-esteem hung on the slender thread of publication, and my style of relating to people was to confront them with myself rather than to seek a connection. At best, I connected through ideas and critical opinions. I had plenty to say about third parties to anybody I considered a friend, but every friend was a third party because no friendship was satisfactory. The practice of criticism itself is an intense form of talking to a third party. Anybody whose parents relayed messages to him or her through others should be adept at third-party communications. In my own case, expressions of support as well as discouragement were rarely overt. One purpose of third-party communications is to minimize responsibility for our feelings and opinions; another is to seek confidence in the illusion of an ally, who becomes a third party under the same conditions that made the alliance seem essential. I have frequently set myself up as a third party to an alliance of two people whom I had considered friends, or allies.

My family of origin consisted of three people who were allied and alienated in various third-party configurations. Not least of these (three) was a dead man, who preceded me in my family trio—he was a powerful third party between me and my mother, but the alliance I sought with him was still far from active. He continued to appear in the form of mentors, but within two years he would erupt from my unconscious as a most astounding personage. In the meantime I bonded with people against my mother in the customary fashion by relating the strange tale of my mother's deception. For me, the third-party design was extremely potent. My mother's great need for an ally had been tragically eroded by her equally great need to make me a third party in her phantasmic alliance with the dead. The suppression of information is of course one of the more virulent strategies of exclusion. Near the end of my mother's life, as I pursued my father back to England, I withheld information from her on the same grounds that she had originally withheld information from me. I didn't trust her enough. I wanted to protect her from the knowledge of an encounter she had always feared for me—the fear that I would be hurt by contacting people who had hurt her. I also wanted to protect myself from the possibility that she might preempt new information that she could somehow use against me once again. Even now, as I struggle to unite my mother and father in the symbolic exercise of biography, I know that the public is my court of appeal, the "ally" I inherited in a case left unresolved by principals now dead.

In the early sixties in New York, my relationship to people underwent a certain change. As a result of knowing Sally and her extended family of friends downtown, I was confronted with feelings and opinions about myself that were not always secondhand. My new life was exhilarating and confusing. Sally and her friends were hosts to a vivid life-style of parties and family camaraderie. In this setting I was known, and accepted, as a critic, but I wanted above all to be integrated as a family member. I had two children and no husband, and I hadn't had anything like a family since the mid-fifties when I was a dancer at the Limón studio.

Much as I participated in the Lower East Side life, I

remained a kind of outsider. The dancers I knew in the mid-fifties weren't really much of a family, but we shared common histories. Elements of my new scene were familiar, but the dominant characteristic of the group was different, specifically in two ways: intimacy was not obscured by manners, and strange behavior was condoned and indulged. About four people constituted the core of this group, and perhaps seven more adhered to it regularly; another fifteen or so were included at any major gathering or party. I was among the seven who clung to the nucleus of the group, spending time with them every day doing things that I formerly had done alone or with my children. In a setting lacking pretense, the way one was as a person was more important than who or what one was in the world. Yet the way one was wasn't defined or limited by manners. To negotiate my presence without manners and without confidence I resorted to buffoonery and self-deprecation; I felt very inferior to the company of my new friends. In this setting I was more of a mother than a critic, and as a mother I was beginning to look unfit. I spent most of my time at Sally's apartment or her friend Charlotte's apartment down the street on East Broadway. They each had two children close in age or not much older than mine.

Already in relation to my friend Marilyn in Washington Heights I had felt inferior as a mother. There I regarded with awe my friend's diligence in structuring her children's time. She was certainly as busy as I was—she danced in Merce Cunningham's company and taught music with her husband in Westchester. The difference between us was that she was much better adapted to her role as a woman. She may not have felt any better about herself than I did, but she was thoroughly motivated to succeed in her role. I had never even been apprised of the role. It was not instilled in me. I imitated my friend to some extent, but my imitations were mere gestures. I bought the same kind of building blocks she had, but I remained aloof from the blocks myself. I set the children up at the sink for "water play" the way she did, but I was unable to enjoy them playing because I was always afraid of the mess they could make. But more to the point, I was incapable of establishing a regimen. I did things more or less on demand or when I felt like it. The worst aspect of this sort of permissiveness or lack of discipline is parental anger. In trying to *avoid* anger (which I associated with discipline), I only brought it on by reacting to the inevitable unruliness accompanying such permissiveness. And I was much more preoccupied with writing than with mothering. Marilyn was my first model mother, the first mother, in fact, besides my own with whom I had ever spent real time while she was functioning as Mother. Clearly it was too late; I was too old to learn and too young to know that I was merely better educated, not more grown-up, than my children. Later on, in 1966, I would suddenly discover, with horror and relief, that my children were intelligent beings. In the meantime I hauled them around with me like so much adorable but difficult baggage. Striving for the best, which seemed beyond my reach personally, I sought out superior environments in which to install myself with them. In a way, we were three stray children, and I was almost conscious of wanting to be adopted by a proper mother. To this end my new friends downtown seemed more available because they were without proper husbands. Though ethnically different from me, their circumstances closely resembled mine. I was a failed bourgeois American, and they were neither from bourgeois families nor from families with bourgeois pretensions. The Lower East Side society was very much a meeting ground for these two types of Americans.

The appeal for a failed bourgeois American like myself of those who were unregenerate and thriving was enormous. These people obviously were enjoying life, yet by middle-class standards they were not supposed to be. They were poor and their prospects were dim because they weren't ambitious.

Or they were ambitious but not driven or imaginative or free enough to set an ambition in motion. Or they were ambitious and their prospects looked good but they were still struggling. The four people who formed the nucleus of the group were not ambitious, although one of them was admirably serving the ambitions of others in his capacity as art dealer: Sally was a dancer, but she spent more time as a mother and person at large than she did dancing. This was even truer of Charlotte, whose ambition to act was not greater than her investment in time spent with family and friends. The other women in this society who had children were, like myself, not willing to sacrifice ambition for motherhood. Actually only four of us fit this category. There were two more, and of these, one was not unlike Sally and Charlotte in her orientation to work and life, and the other was the only mother who appeared to have no ambition of her own. This was Helen Segal, wife of sculptor George Segal. Helen and George lived on a farm in New Jersey; they had two children, and Helen actively served her husband's career besides her role as housewife. Three women in this group who were mothers were successful artists. One was Marcia Marcus, whose time to paint afforded by her husband's mothering of their two children made her a controversial personality. Another was Rosalyn Drexler, whose husband, Sherman, put his wife's career (as artist) before his own. The third was Mary Frank, whose husband, Robert Frank, the filmmaker (along with Alfred Leslie), had brought quite a few of these people together with the beat poets, Allen Ginsberg, Gregory Corso, et al, in a social documentary film called *Pull My Daisy*. That was just before my time, in 1959. One woman besides myself who had children and was serious about work was alone with her children. There were four women without children: two were dancers, who, like Sally, were less interested in making dancing a career than in serving others as teachers; one was an artist who became a successful sculptor in the seventies, and one was a schoolteacher. All the women were Jewish except myself and one other. Sally and Charlotte had grown up in large Jewish families with orthodox parents on the Lower East Side. Charlotte's father was a rabbi who, along with her mother, had disowned her when she was twenty-one for marrying a goy. Sally's parents lived down the street in a housing project and her father sold pretzels in the subway. It was the style and the friendship of these two women that gave the whole East Broadway life its coherence. The art dealer Richard Bellamy, who was living with Charlotte at the time, provided a link to the larger world of rich patrons and the innovative excitement of that period. Bellamy was a failed bourgeois American like myself.

The art world is traditionally host and refuge to misfits from middle-class families. Very few parents of such families encouraged their children to be artists or writers, dancers or composers. In the art world of the sixties, I for one found the kind of serious milieu of displaced people like myself that I would never have imagined existed. These people welcomed individuality and difference; any mark of individuality was valued over the bourgeois criteria of excellence: prosperity, prominence, and correctness. Nonetheless, the people I knew admired any artist who became successful, no matter how grudging their admiration, and they enjoyed certain luxuries that only the rich could provide. They liked being entertained by the rich. They liked meeting each other under the roofs of the rich to dance and drink and dress up. The artists who became rich themselves enlarged the arena in which to masquerade. In this group of beats and hipsters, artists and fallen WASPs, etc., there was actually one bona fide rich man. This was Walter Gutman, who held a very special place as a kind of godfather to the scene. Before I met him, I heard how important he was. He wasn't awesome exactly, but he impressed my friends; one evening, for instance, he had them all picked up in Rolls-Royces and driven to Westchester for a party to celebrate the publication of his book *You Only Have to Get Rich Once*. In 1959, *The New Yorker* published a profile of him, and that year he volunteered to produce *Pull My Daisy*. Walter was a big amiable fellow who was about sixty when I met him. By his age and affluence he seemed an excellent candidate to fill my need for a new paternal model, but while I enjoyed his patronage (he had a small foundation in his own name through which he made tax-deductible grants to his friends downtown) and friendship, I found him too different from myself to excite my paternal myth. His difference was certainly an attraction, and in that he belonged to this entire little society of different people who had captured my imagination and turned my life around, but the attraction of difference is not often a basis for identification. Paradoxically, Walter also made himself too accessible. He was too much one of us. His patronage was not a condition of distance. He liked fraternizing with us and being considered a peer—he was too real to qualify as a model of the proportions I required; the man I needed had to be largely dead—that is, much bigger than life. Walter's background in one or two crucial respects was similar to the rest of ours. He had recently become a sort of failed bourgeois Jew—having reached a certain pinnacle of success as a stockbroker, he had decelerated his life dramatically. Encouraged by his Freudian analyst or analysis, he left his wife of twenty-five years, with whom he had raised three children in Westport, and moved to New York to act out his fantasies. He collected paintings by a number of artists just becoming successful, and he mobilized an old wish to be an artist himself. But the motivation for his new life seemed to lie in an obsession with strong women, specifically of the circus variety—he loved chasing after exotic circus types, especially any woman who could do the one-arm handstand on a slack wire; then he would ask her to model for him. In my opinion, his paintings were more like excuses to court his circus women than the efforts of a serious artist. He also liked female dancers, though I think he much preferred strong arms to strong legs. One woman on the scene who was a favorite was Rosalyn Drexler because she had once wrestled professionally, but Rosalyn was also a good painter and a talented writer, and Walter enjoyed having friends who were accomplished in his own fields. He was certainly a talented writer himself. For several years he had been turning out a stock market letter, which he used as a forum for a running commentary about his life and his interesting friends.

Walter's style was direct and economical, a style I admired myself without the means at that point to be influenced positively by it. I did however involve myself with it in some good-natured but ineffectual capacity as editor. The motivation was money. For three hundred dollars, I posed as an editor of his stock market letter, which he planned to assemble into a book. This was 1963—I was still living in Washington Heights and had met Walter in Woodstock or Provincetown the previous summer. I was hugely entertained by his stories; I'd never known anybody with his kinky interests, or anybody so eager to divulge them—such personal revelations in general were unknown to me. But a lack of secrecy was a hallmark of this milieu. Startlingly different from my background, it was after all a leading attraction for someone like myself who had been the casualty of a big secret. In Walter's case, he seemed to have absolutely nothing to hide, possibly less so than others because of his security as a rich man, and/or his analysis had made him proud of his secrets. In any event, his revelations served to underscore the new-found Bohemianism and individuality in which he was glorying. They were perhaps also the boasts of a man who still needed the conquests of women in one form or another to shore up his identity. I never thought of the women he described as individuals or as people, and neither was I much of an individual to a man like Walter. But I hardly knew myself as an individual; I was barely embryonic that way. I was a kind of voyeur to the individuality of others. As a critic I specialized in detecting the insignia of individuality in art. In relation to someone like Walter, I played the part of a proper woman, reminiscent of a time in my life ten years earlier when I deferred to my philosophy professor. So Walter was, after all, one of my fathers. For about three years, I certainly depended on his interest in me, and while he was not a strong mythological character for me, he enlarged my understanding of what a successful man could be. The other men on this scene were not negligible on this score, but they were much more confusing. I wanted their acceptance and approval, but I was not willing to defer to them to get it. Though I failed to recognize my husband in them—there was a profound superficial difference—they were really so many facsimiles of him in their embattled superiority. These were the totem brothers, a breed that would treat me like an Athene so long as I supported their interests. Besides Walter, three other men close to the East Broadway clan meant something to me at that time.

One was Richard Bellamy, the art dealer, and the others were two of his artists. Of these, George Segal meant more to me as a family man than an artist. He and his wife, Helen, were very hospitable to me and my children; their "farm" in New Jersey was one of my favorite hangouts. George was a stable and amiable patriarch, intellectual and reasonable, not like most of the other male artists I knew. But it was the other male artists whom I chiefly imitated. I identified more with Bellamy and his sculptor, Mark di Suvero. Bellamy was an elegant, mischievous character who constantly eluded my efforts to make me feel worthy of his company. As I've said, like myself he was a failed bourgeois American, though his heritage was more extreme than mine. He had grown up an only child in Ohio with a father of Irish-English descent and a Chinese mother who died when he was seventeen. I loved him for being Chinese, as much because it was impossible to know that he was without having been told as because, once known, it was inescapable in assessing his style. A bizarre travesty of a court jester, eager to please at all costs, but an eagerness—excessive and inappropriate—by which he continually upstaged those he courted; and of an all-American boy, absurdly posturing attitudes of chivalry and executive charm. Bellamy was the first self-conscious stylist, calculated personality, I ever knew; someone whose answer to art was to fashion himself in such an image, he seemed to do nothing not contrived for its effect. The space he occupied was always the site of a ceremonious happening—I never saw him when he wasn't put on. The real Richard, whatever that was, was maddeningly inaccessible, yet delightfully concealed by the ruse of personality. During the sixties, I would come to know others like him. Prior to then, the evasions of truth/dealing with which I was familiar were the standard WASP façades: inscrutability and ambiguity. Saying one thing and meaning another was a specialty of my mother's. Naturally, it was one of my specialties too, so specialized that, like my mother, I never knew myself what I meant. I habitually repressed the unacceptable; a mountain of bad feelings lodged within, surging beneath a mere surface of respectability. The expression of bad feelings was constantly converted into self-effacing niceties, polite complaints, subterfuge, euphemism, deflection, abstraction, projection, social criticism, and so on. I was not altogether unfamiliar with the type of evasion exemplified in Bellamy's antihero personality reconstruction: in boarding school, I had created a rather well-developed clown to front for myself. Since then I had done my best to be a "nice" girl—I never clowned around in New York in the fifties; everyone I knew in the fifties was very serious. Now, in 1961, right out in the so-called real world, people were acting as foolishly as I once had in boarding school. This was a great bonanza for me. I broke out of my garter belts and

knee socks as if I'd been in a maximum security prison for
ten years. I hurled myself at parties and people like a clown
blasted out of a cannon. The artifice of a Bellamy was wasted
on me. Even his prankster aspect was too organized, too
calculated for me. When Bellamy was drunk he turned from
poseur to prankster; when I was drunk I turned from a shy
girl to a noisy brawling exhibitionist. Alcohol was one key to
my new life. Dope was integral to the Lower East Side life,
but others besides myself preferred alcohol. For Mark di
Suvero, it didn't matter much what he used because he was
habitually uninhibited. Mark was my only male friend in the
early sixties. The others were married or attached or homo-
sexual or too young or too old or too famous or something.
I admired a number of them and wanted desperately to get
close to them somehow, but I was not in love with any of
them, and I was certainly not looking for a husband. Anyway, since I served their interests as a critic, I was set apart as
an authority in question. The only male who appeared not to
care was di Suvero.

Mark was the first man I knew whose ambition was accompanied by fearful denunciations of those from whom he
was wresting success. A popular di Suvero story had him in-
stalling his sculpture for a group show at the Whitney
Museum, spying *New York Times* art critic John Canaday,
and lurching over to him bellowing such imprecations as
"*You're* the reason I don't read the *New York Times.*" Mark's
example gave me courage. He was credible enough to give
sanction to outrage. Di Suvero had a huge personality. His
generosity was unbounded, and the noise he made was mega-
sonic. His personal problems were absorbed by social issues,
the target of his rage being the State. Like my other friends
at that time, di Suvero was an American of mixed heritage
whose parents were latecomers. He was born in China himself, a port of call where his parents, both Venetians—one
Catholic, one Jewish—had sought refuge from Italian fascism.

He arrived in San Francisco with his parents, a sister, and two brothers when he was seven. His mother wanted her three sons to be successful in America, and very well they did. I recall the mixture of envy and approval I felt seeing a letter from his mother addressed to "Mark di Suvero, Sculptor." At this time my mother was expressing no interest in my career at all. Fortunately I had been adopted by an extended art family who loved me for my services if nothing else. There was certainly not much else to love me for, because my own good feelings about myself were attached exclusively to my writing. I may not be crediting my friends with a kind of clairvoyance; indeed, I know others saw me as I might someday be, and others saw the daughter my mother once had loved as a child. But whatever they saw that was good was through my own determined efforts to prove I was the bad daughter I thought my mother thought I had become.

Di Suvero's interest in me was complicated by his own serious problems just then, due to a crippling accident that had raised fears about his potency. Three years before I met him, his spinal cord was severed in an elevator shaft mishap. His recovery was considered remarkable—he wasn't supposed to walk again. He was very much walking when I met him, but his leg muscles had permanently atrophied and he was lurching around on braces. His sexual interest was as expedient as mine was, but for a different reason. For myself, any display of male sexual interest that I didn't have to take seriously was a welcome gratuity. For Mark, there were other girls who would take his "problem" more in hand than I could. At any rate our mock interest in one another was the basis for a consortium that I deeply prized. His chauvinism, both male and European, was intense, but in 1963 I was not yet conscious of the social dominance of men, and I was accorded some advantage as a critic. But it was his very chauvinism, coupled with his symbolic emasculation, that held a unique appeal for me. He cut an outrageous figure, towering aggressively over his pathetic legs. If his accident had cut him down to size, it set his masculinity in relief as a study specimen. I couldn't identify it, but I sensed that the real injury here was not to limbs and locomotion but to sexual pride. This was a brooding giant, pondering much more than his own misfortune, disguising his ambition with excessive unseemly behavior. In the early sixties, Mark was a respected sculptor, innovative and influential; a decade later he had overpowered the field, his immense steel girders engraving the sky in many public grounds and cities. He had returned to Venice, the family birthplace, found a young well-born wife there, installed sculptures in various European capitals, brought his Venetian wife "home" to America—all according to the myths of prodigal sons who restore pride to fallen or exiled tribes. His accident, too, seemed such a striking reminder of the maimed hero: Oedipus, and even more so, Hephaestus. In Hephaestus types, here was the real thing. Hephaestus, the god who had been cast down at birth into the sea, was rescued by Thetis, who set him up as a smith. Later, Hera accidentally discovered his workmanship and fetched him back to Olympus where she provided a much finer smithy and arranged for his marriage to Aphrodite. When Zeus was pregnant with Athene, it was Hephaestus who took a "wedge and beetle" and made a breach in his father's skull, permitting the goddess to spring forth, fully armed and with a mighty shout, as the story goes. In 1963 and '64 in New York I played a strange Athene to Mark's Hephaestus. Combining our anxieties and energies, we were capable of making a great spectacle of ourselves around town. But I was not "fully armed" and my "shout" was much more drunken than warlike. Either my birth was fatally premature or the father in question had miscarried me. More likely, a new entrance was in order. I had already found my Zeus in the old philosophy professor in graduate school. Now twelve or thirteen years had passed, and I had engorged myself with culture. It could be said that I was now pregnant with culture. The myth was turning around: The father who had once delivered me was now imprisoned in me, so to speak. It seemed fitting that Mark was my companion just then. In him I saw embodied a tortured, displaced descendant of the Italian Renaissance—a modern Michelangelo running amok in New York, a man with Promethean tools in a land hospitable to foreigners while traditionally stratified for success; but a man in the stratum, the environment, most likely for success, given his background and limitations. In Mark's company the project obviously was storming Olympus. As a social clown, he could disguise his great plans for a coup. More pragmatically, he could discharge the energy he kept under tight control at work, and he was a hard, disciplined worker.

The antisocial male artist has long been an accepted phenomenon. During the fifties, New York had captured the title from Paris as capital of the art world. Denizens of the art world in New York had become familiar with successful male artists, newly arrived, staggering and blustering at such artists' hangouts as the Cedar Tavern on University Place. Jackson Pollock, Willem de Kooning, and Franz Kline were well known habitués. In the early sixties, Max's Kansas City was the favorite artists' bar, a number of artists making deals with the proprietor to exchange their work for free dinners. Mark was just successful enough to command a scene, not yet big enough to compromise his position by an unconsidered visibility. I liked being seen with him because he was very popular, and with his collusion I felt secure in being outrageous. But Mark was also one of my Jewish mothers at that time. His loft on Fulton Street was one of the four hangouts I frequented, with or without my children. With my children, it was better than the park or any playground. Mark was a kind of self-styled social worker. Every week on appointed days he visited a hospital on Rikers Island to encourage crippled or paralyzed friends. Every week also he played host to a group of black boys from the Lower East Side. His loft was a playground of swinging beds and sculptures and crazy objects on wheels made of tires and paint-spattered chunks of metal. Mark loved entertaining children and grown-ups on his mobile assemblages. He whooped and hollered and wildly manipulated these things, milking what he could out of them to simulate the fearful effects of amusement park rides. His serious "public" sculptures always retained some play element, something to climb or swing on or hang from. In the Lower East Side "family," Mark was an affectionate rivalrous sort of big brother, a companion in arms, supportive while secure in his own position, crazy and antagonistic where his sexual anxieties were concerned.

The father figure on this scene was Walter Gutman, but Walter had entered his second (or more advanced) childhood, placing him more or less on a par with the rest of us. George Segal was perhaps more convincing as a father figure, but George was far away in New Jersey and absorbed in his immediate family. The other men were as youthful and insecure in their ways as Bellamy and di Suvero. Sally's husband, Teddy, exemplified the best and the worst of this group. A great hustler, jive artist, master of the put-down, wise child, city slicker, people watcher, hipster at large, Teddy was going nowhere with a lot of style. When I met him, he was or was about to become a junkie; in '66 he jumped or fell from a roof and died. By then the East Broadway society had split apart. Bellamy's artists had become successful and defected to more commercial galleries. As Teddy went down the tubes and Bellamy moved in with Sally, the rest of us took sides and lined up behind Sally or Charlotte. Since Bellamy and myself were competitors for Sally's attentions, I naturally joined Charlotte's camp. Charlotte was suddenly alone, or alone with her three children (the third was Bellamy's), and she was, after all, the woman on this scene who had been designated Mother. But other factors in my life in '63 and '64 determined new alignments with East Broadway friends. A whole different group of people was equally important to me. I belonged really to two families, although the one I've described was much more like home. The second consisted of the artists and choreographers whose work I championed and whose ideas shaped my future. This group contained an updated version of my original dance heroine as well as her counterpart in a male mentor.

Actually my dance figure had split into three versions of herself. In Sally, the dancer was subordinate to mother, teacher, and friend; in this she was closer to my first dance teacher in college, the model for all the rest. Like her, Sally was the doyenne of a new life-style. Sexually, nothing really happened between me and Sally, and not that much more had ever happened with my first dance teacher either. My feeling was as great in the second case as in the first, but in this latest venture the initiative or invitation on the part of my object was missing. I never presumed to take the initiative myself; all my energy was deployed just trying to establish my intentions. At best I believe I signaled my intentions through the flames, so to speak. At length the woman in Boston who had delivered me very graciously extended her hand and invited me to come closer. Closer meant ardent embraces and caresses, never the pursuit of orgasm. Closer was hovering in some rarefied passionate atmosphere between arousal and satisfaction. It remained for the next woman who took me in hand—the woman in Minnesota—to involve my genitals. I found out what an orgasm was and split myself between ideas of pleasure and of the spirit. Thereafter, however, my actual encounters with women ceased. Thus, by 1964, I had been successfully "straight" for twelve years. I had seriously longed for only one woman; I had been celibate (perforce) much of this time, and had had just two meaningful encounters with men, neither of them sexually fulfilling. Obviously after the separation from my husband I wanted to begin all over again and hoped (unconsciously) to be brought out once more. Then, true to form, two women appeared in succession, although the first was a more frustrating variation of the prototype. Sally loved me enough, perhaps, but she was steeped in marital melodramas and diverted by the attentions of our friend the art dealer. Anyway, for her a lesbian event was more of a curiosity than a compulsion, given the moral persuasion of the rising counterculture that anything was possible. At length the invitation was forthcoming in the shape of a challenge, a shape I fearfully declined. The setting was a landing in the stairwell of her apartment building on East Broadway. I was helping her carry laundry bags down her four flights of stairs and berating her for not being intimate enough with me. I had become quite bold—I was becoming outspoken even when sober—and I had been encouraged by Charlotte, who had her own reasons (it presently occurs to me) for seeing my "romance" consummated. As we descended the stairs and reached a particular landing, Sally dramatically (she was very dramatic) hurled her part of the laundry against the wall and spun around in a fiery manner suggesting that we go right back upstairs and do something about it. Naturally her every wish was my command and I obediently followed her back upstairs, but I was much too shaken and nonplused to do anything once we were inside the apartment. I stood transfixed in the middle of the room waiting to see what would happen next. My memory fades quite a bit here, but I know I was flung vigorously, flying perhaps, onto the bed against a wall, where I'm certain we cracked up laughing. Such was life in the shtetl of East Broadway. The upshot of this incident, unfortunately, was a gradual deterioration of our friendship. The way was thus open for the "second woman" in my dyad to bring me out.

In the summer of '64, I produced several dance concerts

at the Washington Square Art Gallery, inviting the choreographers who were in town and whose work I liked to present
pieces there. Among them were the two women who completed this composite dance figure I had dreamed up to represent me in the world. This is not to say that I lacked an
appreciation of male dancers; on the contrary, Merce Cunningham had become my choreographic idol. But my intense
identification with women made me more susceptible to their
total effect on me. I never got close to Cunningham, who
was a lot older and had a peer group of friends, and I never
pursued my connection aggressively or confidently enough to
gain entry to his inner circle. In my dance pantheon he was
the successor to José Limón—both of them had deep roots
in the two great sources of the modern dance tradition in
America. Limón was Doris Humphrey's protégé, and Cunningham had danced with Martha Graham. And since these
two women in turn had danced with Ruth St. Denis, who was
preceded by the great Isadora, I tended to think of the modern
dance tradition in matriarchal terms. It was a woman, too,
who had introduced me to this tradition, and her close female
friend Margaret Lloyd, the dance critic of the *Christian Science Monitor*, who was a torch bearer of the tradition. Limón
had had his day, and now Cunningham seemed (to all the
people I knew, at least) to be in the forefront of the field.
This was 1960–61. Humphrey died in '62, Limón was declining, and Graham was an old warhorse. Cunningham had no
competitors. He had plenty of admirers though, and in '61
his influence was structured through a historic course in
choreography taught at his studio by composer and disciple
Robert Dunn. From this course sprang a whole new wave of
dancing and choreography, launched in a series of concerts at
Judson Memorial Church from '62 through '64. This was the
"movement" I championed as a critic. I was a loud apologist
for Cunningham, but he didn't really need me; by 1963 he
had already looked like an old master, and the establishment

critics were coming around. Then I lost interest when his concerts held no new surprises for me. I forget when that happened exactly, but from the ranks of women in the new Judson scene (a number of choreographers collaborated to present work at each concert), one young woman stood out as a promising heir to the tradition. This was Yvonne Rainer, whose commanding presence and choreographic acumen had roused the whole avant-garde community. Her work instantly bore witness to the past while soundly advancing new ideas. For example, elements in Cunningham's work that were innovative but recessive—a playful use of objects and the incidence of ordinary everyday sort of movement that anybody could do—became capital in Rainer's work. In plotless dancerly "ballets" like Cunningham's, such devices were unknown; they were familiar only in the context of the Dada/surrealist/collage tradition in art, and were now very apparent in the work of Cunningham's contemporaries and friends, Jasper Johns and Robert Rauschenberg. For the Judson choreographers, led by Rainer and at least half a dozen other talented artists, the playful or task-oriented manipulation of objects and the introduction of ordinary everyday movement leaped to the forefront of a new dance aesthetic. I was wildly enthusiastic about this new work; I loved every fresh outrage, and in particular I raved about Rainer, whom I saw inheriting the mantle of Graham and/or Humphrey. I had idolized Humphrey before I was a critic. Now I had that rare opportunity to champion a coterie artist: I could actually participate in establishing a promising dancer. I could share vicariously a success that I myself was helping to promote. The extrusion of another woman into the top level of American dance could be like a fulfillment of service to the memory of my first love. But it was another dancer on this scene, not without great promise herself, who completed the romantic aspect of my dance imago, thus bringing me full circle, for I had not been intimate with one

of that ilk since college. The occasion for this signal event
was a wild party after one of the concerts I produced at the
Washington Square Art Gallery during the summer of '64.

Typically, I had managed to assemble various elements
of my different worlds at this party. I liked imagining that all
the different people I knew should naturally enjoy knowing
each other and persisted in thinking that the art world was
more or less one big happy family. I did take notice of ten-
sions and grievances, especially those directly involving myself, but I never extrapolated any rules of conduct from my
observations; to do that I would first have had to observe
some elementary rules of social conduct—for example, that
someone's degree of prominence affects other people's views
of themselves. Strange as it may seem, it still escaped me that
men in general were prominent while women were not, the
reason being that I had never perceived men and women as
existing in distinct classes. The assumption of male superiority
was so profound that it utterly escaped notice; to notice it
was a breach of conduct. In many parts of the world besides
ours the expression of class or individual superiority is taboo;
pride and integrity are preserved through the avoidance of
invidious comparisons. But of course the very fabric of society
is one of class distinctions, to which we all address ourselves.
In all classes there are two types of people—those who know
their place and those who don't—and among those who
know, there are two kinds of knowing: one tacit and in-
articulate, the other conscious and discriminating. Within
every class, also, in societies like ours there are fluctuating
degrees of mobility, attended by shifting postures, problems
of adaptation, new questions of conduct, and so on. In New
York in the sixties, I happened to be part of a very mobile
crowd. Sex roles were perfectly stable, and the scene was
predominantly white, but there was great movement among
this white male middle class, carrying a few women along
with it. In this company I was dislodged from my moorings,

that is, the place where I knew my place, albeit unconsciously. Suddenly I became someone who did not know her place, and having no *knowledge* of my place, I became an instant anarchist. Only those whose sense of place has been internalized out of habit and programming can move safely into such a dangerous position. Strictly speaking, an anarchist has no (political) objective; loosely speaking, anarchy is a catchword for a stance that veils political ambitions. The men I knew were obviously anarchists in this latter sense. I should add, though, that there were men on the scene like myself, whom I tended to discount because only the ambitious ones interested me. I'm not, however, discounting the ambition inherent in the passive position, only stressing the difference in orientation.

The most outstanding man in this flowering avant-garde perfectly illustrated the tactic of mobility employed by class(less) groups of white males. The head honcho of the Neo-Dada movement, the guiding intellect behind a broad spectrum of antiestablishment aesthetics, was Merce Cunningham's friend and composer, John Cage. Cage urged anarchy, built anarchy into the method and structure and teaching of his work, all the while establishing himself king of the latest word in anarchy, if you will. His ambition was very clear. Once he told me, smiling broadly and mischievously, "We're going to change all that"—referring to the status quo in music. I loved it. I thought he really could do it. I was as eager to help him as I was to establish Rainer. I never noticed that avowed purposes were often belied by strong social mobility. Obviously I was still vulnerable to a living viable male mentor—in this I joined the great majority of artists I knew then. Cage was our leader, who would carry us to the top or remain safely isolated from the mainstream. With the rest of the men, with a few exceptions, I behaved in a classless and therefore objectionable manner. They had all become clones of my estranged husband; like him, they were at once companionable and murderous. I was like a younger sister who had never been broken, a condition tolerable only through the power of my position as a critic. Either to counteract my position and/or to express the faith I still really had in the system I was attacking (along with my male friends), I protected myself by appearing in the degraded form of a drunken fool. I never actually thought "Now I'm going out to get drunk and act like a fool in order to throw them off" or anything like that; I think I merely sensed that I had to undermine my threat, and I had to unload the burden and tension of compromise in some arena associated with its origin. In the summer of '64, as the result of the party after a Washington Square Art Gallery concert, I lost my protection. To at least one element of my male peer group I committed a grave offense—I usurped their feeling that they had a right to the most desirable women on the scene.

Nothing was secret or sacred in the little world I moved around in. The dancer who had selected me to be her first "older woman" was only twenty-four, nearly a virgin, and quite a beautiful specimen of WASP American pulchritude. In fact, I soon learned that she was considered the Garbo in our midst. I also learned, to my surprise, that she had been regarding me from afar as an objective for six months. The first time I noticed her or her interest in me was at this drunken party. Then I promptly fell in love. No woman had touched me in twelve years. The past, in fact, was catching up with me in various ways. This period approaching the mid-sixties was not unlike a time of disintegration seven years earlier; the "dream figures" (the people in my life) were transposed in unfamiliar combinations, but the story was essentially the same. Nothing had really changed—the cast of characters had simply expanded, and the arena for action was transformed. The changes were radical differences in appearance, and a heightened expression of my central conflict, changes that augured the possibility of real change. By "real change" I mean the prehension of a given life, the factors and influences that shape it, the reactions and adaptations to it, the patterns or repetitions inherent in it—insights providing a means to alter and control things and have them go differently if so desired.

Changes of heart may suffice completely. Agencies of change are the subject of a vast world literature, to which I add my own story. The sixties was a time rife with change, notorious in agencies of the occult and for madness and civil disruption. The updated libretto of my life was amplified by world events and an accumulation of years that had coiled into something called a midlife crisis. The signs of breakdown were familiar; the resolution of seven years earlier—a conventional marriage—was not an available option anymore. Preceding my new exciting misalliance, I had made similar desperate demonstrations of faith in my role as a woman. I was even dressing up in drag. Ransacking the thrift stores with my new friends downtown, I found clothes that made me feel like a "woman" for the first time—floppy hats, feather boas, worn velvet things, vampy vintage dresses, flamboyant patterned stockings—in these sorts of costumes I careered around town, party hopping and getting into all sorts of trouble. The prevalent role/image of women in that group was the artist's moll, a chippie who was wife, mistress, or free agent. I was living with two children and I did my best to look available, though I was truly interested in just my friend Sally and went to bed only with strangers. Such encounters were rare, but the outcome of one of them was strikingly reminiscent of my crisis of 1956. At that time also I was having an unrequited affair with a dancer and sometimes sleeping around with strange men. Then, as now in 1963, I used a pregnancy to smoke-screen my true interests and to focus attention on my plight, that is, on myself.

For old images in men I now reached even further back than in 1956—my new candidate for trouble was a college student no older than my boyfriend had been in boarding school, and similarly dark and short. As in '56, the abortion was prolonged by a dilation procedure involving more visits than one and culminating in a spontaneous "miscarriage." Similarly also, I ended up at the hospital, in this case the one where my children had been delivered (formerly, the one where my mother had trained as a nurse), and a woman I was close to accompanied me to both places—to the abortionist, then to the hospital. I also got my money back. In the fifties my friends had paid the abortionist, and later I pursued the man who was responsible to compensate all of us. Reenacting my outrage, in the sixties I collected from the abortionist after three visits to him produced no results; I did this following a bus trip to Pennsylvania to see the famous Dr. Spencer, who made an appointment for the next week. Then, within a day or two, I miscarried spontaneously. I never related the two events, separated in time by merely seven years. I only related events like these by noting that I was getting along as badly as ever. Soon I was getting along worse than ever before. I was "out" sexually, but there, with my new partner, I was completely isolated. There were no women together in this scene whatsoever, and since I was not "out" in my head, I myself disapproved of what I was doing. I know I disapproved by the way I acted, not by what I was thinking—I had no thoughts of a social/personal/political nature. The way people often got together in those days reflected this kind of ignorance. The background for a new "marriage" was frequently a drunken party—the idea was to wake up the next morning with your new intimacy, preferably someone you hardly knew but who was known on the scene. My two significant relationships in the sixties commenced this way; the second person was not even known at large but somebody I met on the street outside a bar.

Such "chance" meetings clearly represent an abdication of responsibility. If social barriers inhibit certain intimacies, a loss of social control may facilitate them. Alcohol of course is not the only medium for easing contacts between the socially estranged. Age is a traditional solvent—that is, an "older woman" may sanction the forbidden liaison. And between women, a man has often mediated their encounter, unwittingly or by arrangement. Both of my chance meetings in the sixties were mediated by a man. By some prescience I asked Mark di Suvero to host a party at his loft after that summer concert in '64. Sally was there, and other elements of the East Broadway gang, and the Judson vanguard. Thus the man and the woman who meant most to me at that time presided, in a sense, over my new connection. That doesn't mean I had their blessing. On the contrary, in Sally's case a certain defection was naturally assumed, and I no doubt exulted to myself over what I thought was my good fortune. In Mark's case I continued loping along, pursuing his company, bringing my new companion along with me. His attitude was a heightened expression of sexual buffoonery. It was from another quarter in this circle that I had something to worry about. By late fall that year my relationship was virtually under siege. The final phase of my life as my mother's daughter, or son, the "first life" we all lead in a society in which the father is transcendent, was drawing swiftly to a close.

My mother herself at this time was living in quasi-retirement in the country in Connecticut. She had by then really retired from my life, and was involved in it only to the extent she needed to be in order to see her grandchildren. I made one effort to interest her in my career: sometime in the summer of '63 I brazenly showed her an issue of *Harper's Bazaar* with a small photo of myself in it (accompanying an article I had written about Happenings), and she set it aside without comment, evidently affronted. It never occurred to me that she feared for my children and condemned me as a mother, nor I suppose did it occur to her that if I were more of a mother she wouldn't be able to think of the children as hers to the extent that she did. But I think we both wanted it both ways: I wanted her to appreciate me as a writer and accept me as a mother, and she reserved the right to judge me as a mother regardless of her interests to the contrary. Since I had lost the protection of a husband, she naturally concluded that it was impossible for me both to be a proper mother and pursue a career. She was perfectly right of course. Even with the protection of a husband I hadn't been equipped to be a proper mother, though my mother was prepared to regard me as one (and even accept me as a writer) while I remained married. Security and appearances were everything to my mother. They were everything to me too, but having lost them, I was still basically the same kind of mother. Nonetheless I must have shared my mother's opinion that in the eyes of the world I wasn't, and my downgraded circumstances seemed to support that view. I was living on Houston Street in a small railroad flat over a tombstone business, and I was beset with difficulties. The daily round was never a cause for being creative, but rather an obstacle to a better life elsewhere. "Elsewhere" was wherever the parties and exhibitions were. A car was more important to me than food or furniture. A baby-sitter was more valuable than all the diamonds in Africa. A collective of women in circumstances similar to mine would obviously have made things easier; the collective I had was informal and friendly, not based on a recognition of mutual need. Judgment rather than action naturally obtained in a scene still guided by conventional values. And this was eminently true also of the feeling that existed between my mother and me. Underlying the whole fabric of life at that time was the judgment that things were not right. The possibility of creative action was precluded by judgments based on accepted values. Improvement in a scenario that was inherently wrong socially was inconceivable. My mother herself had already tried and failed at her own independent solution to parenthood; her judgment of me was the same she applied to herself. The difference between us was in form and degree, not in essence. We now played out a curious variation of the arrangement my mother had had with my grandmother when I was small. This time two other people were involved, my ex-husband and his new wife, providing us with an opportunity to double up on our roles. In relation to me, my mother could play her mother—suspicious and critical—while understudying my job during the summer months. In relation to my ex-husband and his new wife she played herself when she was younger and wanted access to her daughter, in this case her granddaughter and grandson. And I now acted out with my mother—visiting her to see my children—the same role she once had acted out with her own mother. The shift involving the children's father occurred the year I was living alone with them, '63–'64, on Houston Street. Until then he saw them irregularly on Sundays, increasingly over weekends. Now, with a young woman who took a motherly interest in them, he suggested taking them four days a week while I kept them three. A year later the shift was complete, and I became a Sunday parent myself. There was never any legal business between us regarding money or custody, there were just plenty of bad feelings. My mother was ever eager to take over my role, yet grateful that the children had a new mother married to their father. Among the four adults, only the new mother/wife was (tacitly) accredited by all. I still had a very low opinion of the boy I had married, and my mother had never liked him; she only liked him in his role of husband. But as we were unable to dispense with him—in fact, there was no reason to suppose he might not be a better father than husband, especially with a woman he liked better than me, and who would assume so much maternal responsibility—we had to continue to take his feelings about us into account. This did not make my mother and me allies. Essentially, she agreed with the children's father and his wife that I was a failed mother, a condition precluding any recognition of career. Thus, from their point of view, I was nothing. And I agreed with my ex-husband and his wife that my mother was crazy. By 1964 I had the "modern" attitude toward my mother that her machinations over my father were Victorian and outlandish, but what I was really agreeing with was a view of my mother that accounted for the way I was. In other words, I was (as) bad (as my mother) because she had made me that way. As outsiders in a new family dynamic, my mother and I struggled in our own fashion to keep up with the children. She was very aggressive about continuing to have them in the summer and take them special places during the year and unhappy when she encountered resistance from their father. I was very dutiful about seeing them once a week wherever they were and unhappy about an attitude toward myself that I accepted. Eventually all this changed and the children even came back to me, creating strange and unprecedented convolutions in the family mode. . . . In the meantime, in 1964, midway between solutions, the children uptown four days a week and downtown three, the picture was complicated by the addition of my own young woman to the ménage on Houston Street.

My new friend drew me toward several extremes of my personality. Since she was beautiful, in the accepted *Vogue* sense, I was more decidedly funny-looking myself. To the degree that falling in love is a projection of qualities thought to be missing, I had fallen abysmally in love. This young woman was to all immediate appearances everything considered desirable by WASP American standards. Standards of maturity, integrity, character, and so on, were not considerations then, at least not by me and the people I knew. Glamour, fame, individuality, creative talent or genius— these were the values prized by the art world of the sixties in New York. For my Lower East Side friends, personal health and physical-mental-sexual well-being was a greater priority. The women in particular were involved in various therapies, and the ones who were dancers were ultimately more interested in dancing for health than for creative recognition. For my dancer friends in the ambitious performing crowd, health was a professional necessity, not a goal in itself, in the sense that a sound physical state enhances the quality of life and of living together. The glamorous theatrical aspect of life was inverted between these two groups: the professionals dressed up (or down, the vanguard style was spare) for performance; the Lower East Side women, in general, dressed for the street and the parties. Everybody loved the parties. Most of the women I knew downtown liked being seen in flamboyant outfits, and I had adapted myself to this dress code. I had several really ridiculous costumes; I enjoyed feeling absurdly resplendent. I got this sense that a costume alone was proof of womanhood; any deficiency felt or imagined as a woman could be camouflaged and redeemed by ladies' drag. Obviously I was a kind of male transvestite in this period, one who loved being taken for a woman. However, I quickly reverted to my nondescript asexual uniforms in the company of a beautiful girl whose style was plain.

The center of my allegiance now shifted to the more ambitious group of dancers whose work I reviewed. At the same time I remained deeply impressed by the counter-culture values of East Broadway. My new romance brought me back to issues that had been unresolved in boarding school. As a girl I had come full circle, and then some. Having left school and turned into a dancer, then into a wife and mother, and finally into a floozie, I was now ready to be a boy again. My life as a female impostor had not been very successful. In my final "transvestite" phase I had even presented myself in concert, performing in events by others or of my own making. One such event was quite gratifying from an infiltrator's point of view. Having spied me at a Christmas party in a loud red dress and black filigree stockings, my artist hero John Cage asked me to join him and his colleague David Tudor the next spring in performing the "dancer" part in a piece of his called *Music Walk*. This was 1962, during the height of my espousal of his cause. Within the ten-minute limit of this piece, I was allowed to do what I wanted, with the understanding that I submit my materials to the chance procedures of his score. By these procedures I would determine the sequence and time/length of my activities. I dutifully made my score from his, each of a group of forty or more three-by-four cards identifying an action and its time condition; then at the rehearsal the cards were more or less ruined when I dropped them in some water, so I abandoned them at the performance and improvised my part. In this ten-minute period I managed to present together my three female travesties: the hoyden, the dancer, and the wife-and-mother. Wearing my loud red dress and my stockings, I executed a number of household chores—cleaning a baby bottle, vacuuming, frying bacon, pulling a vehicular toy dog on a string, and so on—stopping long enough downstage to perform a slinky sort of dance plastique. The mess I usually made in these roles and outfits was here contained by an authority I had never internalized. The only domain I had arrogated to myself for working this all out was my writing. By standards of mental health, in lieu of conventional therapy, these public messes were curative signs, even if socially damaging, but signs they remained. Of all the people I knew, only my friend Charlotte tried to tell me something about myself. After one party freak-out or another where I hung upside down from the rafters or pipes and lost or ripped or injured things and remembered very little, Charlotte might gently suggest that I was disturbed. I think I suspected she was right, but I was having too much fun to do anything about it. At any rate, after one final fling in the fall of '64,

I drew back—fatally, it could be said—from these excesses. The reason was that I was living with a very controlled, rather severe sort of person who was a commanding performer; or more tellingly, a person whose female authenticity, in the socially accepted sense, caused me to withdraw my own parodies and let her carry the projection.

True to my whims, that fall I accepted an invitation to perform in a big sprawling Happening by composer Karlheinz Stockhausen at Carnegie Recital Hall. Many artists performed in this piece, called *Inside Originale*, and I played a part designated "free agent." There were no such limits as obtained in the Cage piece. Five nights in a row I appeared quite drunk in outlandish female accouterments and hung upside down from a scaffolding and did my best to disrupt the performances of the other artists involved. Several sensitive artists were offended or outraged; only Allen Ginsberg, who was reading his poetry, was forbearing, and as usual I tried to resolve my feelings by analyzing the event for my newspaper. Thereafter for the rest of the year I played the critic, looking more like a boarding school girl on vacation, a little jaded, worn, depleted, but still very shy and tentative, not the least bit more confident than when I was in school. But I was not nearly so well off. While a relationship with some ideal projection of myself (the "real girl" I loved at St. Mary's) was at last consummated, the setting for this event was no longer protective. I had long ceased living exclusively with women, in whose company I had succeeded as a boy without being condemned as a girl. Now, as a boy, out in the real world with "real boys," I lost my credibility in both sex roles. I was hardly a boy in a world that defined me as a girl no matter what I did to the contrary. And having abdicated my pretense at being a girl, I was exposed to being considered a fraudulent boy. This was the problem I had once attempted to resolve by my marriage.

A fraudulent identity is not always cause for concern or reform. It can also be the target of good fun, and it has always provided an occasion for successful disguise. Neither of these treatments was possible in 1964 in a milieu in which I had too much power to be considered good fun and in which my interests were too well known to make my new liaison appear harmless. The art world was, and I suppose always has been, deceptively laissez-faire—a certain Bohemian disregard or acceptance of the different life-styles of its denizens could be misleading. In particular, nothing is so taken for granted in the art world as the traditional sex roles. The bourgeois values of "artistic" middle-class misfits or dropouts were never impaired by simple differences in appearance. A shift in the arena of struggle for success is only in fact a denial of appearances (that is, the parental estates as they seem), not of basic values. And since this new arena is so fraught with uncertainty, its indicators of success so unreliable, basic assumed values can be more desperately prized than they are "back home." Males in this fluid and dubious society may be especially dependent on the support of women, which they derive as their right. A number of women I knew in the sixties doubled as wife and artist's assistant. Only a couple of women in the sixties in New York attained prominence as painters or sculptors—I saw many women with excellent or promising work that was bypassed or ignored. Women as dancers, on the other hand, were traditionally encouraged. Dancers were always big game in the sex field. The dancer who got me thought I was big game as a critic; the other dancers in our world thought their colleague had made a mistake. On the whole, dancers were enamored of male artists, and male artists traditionally love dancers, male or female. But in addition to mistaking my gender, my beautiful dancer friend had abused rules of peerage. And as a critic I could now be seen in a certain nepotistic light. None of this was either clear or discussed, at least by me or my friend; there was simply an atmosphere, from which events and messages would occasionally crystallize.

My friend's intimate circle of artistic collaborators was

in Europe when we got together. Their absence had something to do with our connection. The godfather and patron
to this group was the painter Robert Rauschenberg, who
since 1956 had been collaborating closely with Merce Cunningham as set designer and stage manager. Their association
lasted until 1965, but Rauschenberg's ascendancy as a major
American painter was established in 1961 with a retrospective
of his work at the Jewish Museum. I first saw something of
his at a show of sixteen painters at the Museum of Modern
Art in 1960 and was very impressed to see this big, sloppy
sort of painting with an old work shirt stuck in it. I hadn't
been so pleasurably taken aback since first seeing Jackson
Pollock's work in the fifties. I loved being affronted and
captivated at the same time and was greatly in awe of both
Rauschenberg and Jasper Johns, who were always mentioned
in the same breath. As we peeled into the sixties they had
huge reputations. I heard that they had been very poor, and
now they had Jags and maids and white suits and they owned
big buildings and all. American painters were coming of age.
The first wave of truly successful painters, in the fifties, hadn't
been so stylish; Rauschenberg and Johns mixed easily with
the rich and the powerful. These two men were also very
different from each other, as I discovered much later on, but
at the time I lumped them together with Cunningham and
Cage as a kind of quadrumvirate—four grand old men of art,
influential and successful and way out of my reach. Cage was
no older than fifty, Cunningham somewhat younger, Rauschenberg was only a few years older than me, and Johns a
year younger, but I thought of them all as much older.

Of the four, I only tangled with Rauschenberg because in
'63 he appeared as a heavy on the Judson Dance Theater
scene, which was my own preserve. While he continued de-
signing for Cunningham and touring with him, his interest
was drawn to the Judson choreographers through his friend
Steve Paxton, a dancer in the Cunningham company who was

a founder of the Judson Dance Theater. Rauschenberg was a showman; his work was always bold and theatrical, and the Judson situation, so committed to work by nondancers as well as dancers, gave him an opportunity to perform. Quite a few poets, painters, composers, and sculptors appeared in, or made, dances that were shown in Judson concerts; I was one of these "nondancers" myself. But Rauschenberg was instantly different from the rest of us. Wherever he appeared, he dominated the company with his engaging personality and confidence. Moreover he brought his huge art world reputation with him. Almost as soon as he appeared as a performer, the complexion of the Judson scene changed. The big sprawling concerts at the church involving lots of people continued to take place, but Rauschenberg (with Paxton) became the center of a small elite group that performed in other settings under art world auspices. Paxton often played entrepreneur, organizing concerts through Rauschenberg's connections. Looking back, it seems almost as if a company had been casually formed, but never named or identified as such, from the best resources of young Judson talent. Besides Paxton, the core of Rauschenberg's group consisted of Alex Hay and Deborah Hay, who were vital contributors to the new choreography. Alex Hay was a painter primarily, but his choreography was outstanding. The four performed in works by each other, but concerts under the auspices of Rauschenberg and/or Paxton always included seven or eight other artists whose work was special, most notably Yvonne Rainer, sculptor Robert Morris (then living with Rainer), David Gordon and Valda Setterfield, Trisha Brown, and Lucinda Childs. These were the "beautiful people" of that far-flung scene; in a high school popularity contest, they would have been the winners. This was a collective of artists, several of whom made work specifically opposed to principles of stardom and hierarchy. Yet certain individuals were undeniably brilliant and were independently ambitious as well. And since Rauschenberg was already a star, whatever he did was considered interesting; his very presence belied, or undermined, the open, inclusive nature of the Judson movement. The glamour of his connections was very seductive, and he was a grand party-giver himself. His presence posed a fair conflict for me. I was attracted to him and his work and what he represented, and at the same time threatened by it. Had I thought it through, I would have wished him back on his own territory, where I could continue to admire and distance him, the way I did his colleagues Cage, Cunningham, and Johns. Now I felt constrained to dislike someone I admired, simply because he disliked me, or, more accurately I'm sure, had no use for me. The people Rauschenberg appeared (to me) to like were good-looking, talented male or female dancers, those who might be athletes and cheerleaders in another setting; this was still a very sexist little society, after all. Yvonne Rainer, whom Rauschenberg once described as "formidable," and who was as ambivalent about him as I was, passed by his standards because of her qualifications as a performer. At close quarters I was confronted with a powerful male who regarded me askance. So long as he found me unacceptable, I resented his power, and I hated resenting someone I admired.

Critics in general were, as ever, an abhorred species; most critics stay in their place apart from the scene or artists they review. The artists in this group tried to force this on me by excluding me as a performer. I had other opportunities to prove myself as a performer, but I never took performance seriously enough to overcome the resistance of my artist friends. If I was trying to prove anything, it was perhaps to reassure the group that I wouldn't challenge their perception of me as critic and outsider, and since I was afraid to perform, I usually performed drunk and therefore was considered an unreliable performer.

I had one glorious moment as a drunken performer when a certain event I created satisfied both the need to do something that looked good and the need to be held in contempt by other "serious" performers. This was back in '63. The setting was the Pocket Theatre on Third Avenue, where a number of us contributed individual events to a full evening. I constructed an "English Country Garden" in which a violinist named Malcolm Goldstein sat on a chair on stage playing the song by that name over and over while I stood nearby in a tub of water full of artificial flowers, wearing black boots, slicker, and slicker hat, and Robert Morris approached me from the back of the theater, walking down the aisle wearing a voluminous sheet with the word "HILL" printed on a placard around his neck. When he reached the tub he stood on a chair next to it and poured water over my head from a watering can he was carrying under the sheet. Then, with great relish and abandon, I threw the artificial flowers into the audience. The audience was delighted, and I had a wonderful time—I'd been drinking all day in a neighborhood bar with George Brecht. The event was controlled by its own design, and my need to make a mess was satisfied by an overflow of water all over the stage, enraging David Gordon and Valda Setterfield, whose number was next. I rushed around with a mop trying to clean it up, but the damage was really an impropriety. Afterward Brecht and I and some other fun-loving friends repaired to an Egyptian belly-dancing establishment on Eighth Avenue, where at some point I stood on a table pretending to be Isadora in Paris; the rest of the night was spent in the back of my car with Brecht on the Lower West Side.

Obviously I was a soloist then on stage as in life. I had few complementary understandings with people at that time, so that besides being a critic, which already set me apart, I was an isolated sort of person, squared off against the world through my inability to make contact with it. One reason I became a critic must have been to explore this remote position. And as if that were not enough, during this period, like

Rauschenberg and Paxton, I played entrepreneur, producing concerts starring of course the same choreographers, including Paxton. I hardly need say that an undercurrent of struggle existed between us. I was unhappy about this conflict, but I repressed it because I couldn't deal with it or change it. In my personal life I always assumed the status quo, in which I always played the wronged party. The model for this viewpoint, the relationship between me and my mother, had long congealed. Any feeling I had that I was *unjustly* wronged was redirected, sublimated, in my aggressive activities. These activities in turn, of course, reinforced my sense of alienation. The thing that kept me going was the knowledge that these people needed me; they may not have liked me, but they liked my criticism, or at least depended on the publicity. Rauschenberg didn't need me because he was an established painter, and his investment in performance work was not any greater than mine. Here was the rub. We were both Sunday performers with opposing claims to a group of up-and-coming artists. But through Paxton he had become integral to the group, or an elite part of it, while I remained tangential. That could have changed when they were all away in Europe the summer of '64 touring with Cunningham, and I fell into bed with one of their own who was left behind, but this only made matters worse. To find a favored party of their group in bed with the critic, who was moreover the wrong sex, was a territorial affront. I never thought of it that way, indeed I don't believe I thought of it at all, but the air was charged with the feeling of my being wrong and excluded. I was right in the middle of everything; the parties and concerts brought us together all the time, yet I was unable either to join them or to hold my own. To join them would have meant abjuring any sovereignty I felt. To hold my own I would have had to feel more like a boy, and to join them concede that I was a girl. I was, in effect, neither. But I was not alone in my isolation. While my new friend's beauty and talent made her an acceptable girl, and she was appropriately demure, she was not a joiner any more than I was. She was not necessarily the girl she appeared to be, and she was hardly a boy, psychologically speaking, at the embryonic age of twenty-four. She was perhaps a younger version of myself, a different model of the type, stranded between genders, trying out solutions as creative as the problem, but in a social context that had already damned the problem. After a short period of grace, the wrath of the patriarchy, a condition and prejudice within as well as without, was upon us.

8

Halcyon
and Light Blue

This was an extraordinary year for me because for the first time I was openly flouting my mother's way of life, thus leaving me prey to my own opposition. By my mother's way of life I mean her successful suppression of damaging information about herself, and her successful protection of a forged identity. The heavy price she paid for this way of life is endemic to my story but not to my immediate point. The identity my mother had forged depended completely upon my collusion as the innocent party. I was the living proof of her upgraded status as the widow of a mysterious Englishman. My mother was not a novelist—it would never have occurred to her to merely invent an identity like this. She had to have a proper pretext for it. What better than the "hell" that "hath no fury like a woman scorned"! The choice of a man unwilling to marry her, and indiscreet enough to make her pregnant, thus compromising his social position, was all my mother needed to justify borrowing an identity that she couldn't or didn't want to come by legally. The use of a child in property deals is intrinsic to civilization; the use my mother made of me was a recourse of "the second sex," a deadly and curious expedient, not very well understood. (The use of bastard sons by fathers is another tradition, one we know more about from a close reading of history.) For my mother

I was a baby hostage, the property by which she secured an identity, only to be given up (to the patriarchy) under conditions that the patriarchy could never confirm. In a scheme like this my marriage was a brief aberration. In attempting to escape my mother's claim, I submitted to the very forces that opposed her use of me, that is, my birth. Nonetheless, by surviving that dangerous adventure, and presenting my mother with a granddaughter, I was now relatively free to live my own life. At this moment it could be seen that I was awash in a world in which I had outlived the purpose that had brought me there—I had to invent myself now or never at all. As my mother's hold on me loosened, I acted more and more like an abandoned child; she had released me, but I had nowhere to go. Moreover, her releasing me was subject to the understanding that I remained an embarrassment to her, but should never openly embarrass her.

The question of my mother's salvation is critical in assessing her attitude. In any story like this a strong counter-movement exists to redress wrongs, to make reparations and unite what has been put asunder. A kind of psychic undertow acts against the "visible" part of the story, an undertow with its own life and stratagems. My mother's control over me as an adversary was the strategy by which she hoped (unconsciously) to be acquitted. As an ally I was no longer much use to her. I knew her story, but nobody else (in her world, the *only* world) did, and I would never tell them or embarrass her in their presence. She was stuck with her story. She might have to die with it. By 1964 I was completely divided in my loyalties—to my mother and myself. To the extent that I was still her ally, I was that far from exonerating her, and I was a long way off. A certain midpoint in our struggle had been reached, that axial moment when the lines of dramatic conflict are clearly delineated, yet far from resolved. A keen observer of our struggle could have identified its course and predicted its outcome. My mother and I were acting our parts in separate arenas, each unaware that a mutual project was the cause of everything we did. She had no way of knowing that her "baby hostage"—now out on her own—was busy establishing a forum in which to expose her "brutal treatment in captivity." The art world in New York meant nothing to her; its capabilities for publicity were unknown to her, nor were they known to me, except insofar as I learned mindlessly how to use them. The route I had chosen, or happened by, was open rebellion. By living frankly with another girl—a scandal in the small society I inhabited—I had ceased living my mother's way of life. The suppression of damaging information was essential to this way of life; a failure to do so could mean social death. I had never lived with a girl, I hadn't slept with one in twelve years, yet now I appeared to be flaunting a relationship that struck at the heart of the patriarchy. Soon a knight from this establishment appeared to challenge my audacity.

This "knight" was not an extrusion of our immediate group of artists and choreographers; he came rather from the ranks of pop or op artists loosely associated with the Lower East Side society through their dealer, Richard Bellamy. In 1964 he was an overnight success, a wunderkind, a rich and influential figure at twenty-five. His paintings were among the most striking and original of the "color field" specialists: big, clean-looking canvases, small oval shapes of one color distributed on some invisibly rigged mathematical grid over a single color ground, smashing optical effects. A small round-shaped sort of huggable-looking guy, dark and quiet, shy yet aggressive, appearing everywhere in paint-spattered work clothes; he owned a whole building and drove a motorcycle. His wife was also dark and adorable, and she managed his affairs and helped him paint his paintings. But success in the art world as in other entertainment worlds often means the end of a marriage. The end in this case must have occurred when the boy in question fell in love with my girl friend.

Sometime in the fall of '64, my relationship was put on notice, so to speak. I could have been living with a grown-up daughter besieged by the favors and demands of a serious suitor; as a lover I had that much credibility. The only respect for relationships like ours was by default, through lack of interest. I had no real respect for the relationship myself, but I was very interested in it. For me a relationship was something social (marriage) or economic (boss/labor), or something between friends, things that came ready-made or were available for use like husbands or ministers or TV sets; I respected a relationship according to its assumed hierarchical value. The relationship I was having had no assumed value whatever, and I had no reason to think differently from everybody else. But I had a subversive sphere of value that depended on my alter-identity as a boy. I saw myself living with a beautiful girl whom any boy would love to have; I saw myself as "any boy" who would be very jealous of such a relationship. So I was quite possessive and proud, and therefore just as affronted and murderous. I clung desperately to the relationship while expertly colluding in ending it. I crashed into myself all year long, and in the end I got the better of me because I knew I should be taken for what I was or was supposed to be, that is, a girl. In the form of my girl friend I had an appropriate stand-in with a man, and I encouraged this rape of the relationship, by no other means than my fierce attention to it. To be affronted by the assault on the relationship was to be affronted by the relationship itself, which I fully agreed was no good. It had to be overthrown. And I had to resist the assault. This is the game called love (and/or war) when love is still merely possessive. And like a girl I focused more on the relationship than on the means by which I had obtained it, that is, my work. More like a boy, my girl friend increased her attention to her work, her choreography; a girl friend for me would always be somebody like my mother who went to work. I never had a girl friend who, like myself, was a girl without a father. I wanted girls who had fathers, a girl like my mother. I was not doing girlish work exactly, but I was doing it at home. I hated appearing on the premises of my publications; I was still only comfortable publicly when drunk. At home I was only comfortable when working. I loved my relationship (I was "in love" with it) but I was incapable of loving anybody. A relationship for me was still a social (or economic) event, not a cause for care, affection, support, compassion, and so on; not something to create, like an artwork, or nourish, like a plant. After our romance subsided, the relationship became a cause for struggle—relationships defined chiefly by hierarchical values are necessarily limited by struggle. The agreement to set roles—one dominant, one submissive—is what keeps the hierarchies going. We're born into the roles, or we apply to fill them; we fight to keep them, or try to change them. The art society I inhabited was very mobile, an excellent arena in which to act out a chapter of my real struggle, that with my mother. If I were my mother, and the young painter who fell in love with my girl friend were my ex-husband, I must have been furious when he came to get my daughter, that is, me. Yet I would have concluded that she would do best to go with him. I played all the parts. Incidents of violence common in my marriage once again marked my life. The stage sets for my affair were the flat on Houston Street, the streets at large, theaters and galleries, strange houses in other cities. The knight on shining motorcycle in paint-spattered work clothes followed us everywhere.

While he concentrated on my girl friend, his dealer attempted to run interference for him, to tackle or sack the competition, as the football people say. The war cry that heralded these exercises, improvised and sporadic as they were, was perhaps a remark our friend and dealer made to me one day to the effect that I was corrupting the young. No other remark was ever made, there were just "incidents."

Only one such incident occurred in a setting where the four of us congregated together; for the others, the dealer and myself were alone. Once apparently I provoked an attack just by getting into a taxi with him, an occasion upon which he put out a cigarette on the back of my hand. One other time I did the same by walking into his gallery, whereupon he tied me up with rope to a chair. At the time I didn't link this sort of attention with the campaign to seize my girl friend, or I should say I did, but not consciously. Had I known what was going on, I doubt I would have been so exposed. I think I felt amused and flattered and terrified and baffled and appalled. On one occasion, in Hartford, I was thoroughly outraged because I thought he seriously meant to kill me. That was the time when we were all together. The excuse to converge was a concert in which my friend performed with other Judson choreographers. Afterward, at a party at a rich patron's house, the dealer brandished a big kitchen knife, threatening to carve me up with it. Possibly I provoked the attack just by talking to him, and/or by challenging him on something he said, feeling bold because we were surrounded by people. This was surely reminiscent of my being chased down a street by my husband wielding a toilet plunger several years earlier.

Parties in the sixties were murky with alcohol and frequently studded with violence. Happenings and art events were themselves often characterized by violence. Later on, by 1966, this tendency actually crystallized in a movement called Destruction Art. Perhaps I may have preferred to imagine that the art dealer's attacks were just Happenings. A certain confusion of art and life was peculiar to the aesthetic of the times; I was enthralled by this confusion—for me it was a therapeutic confusion that eventually caused me to pay more attention to life. The inclusion of so much life in art, the use, say, of "found objects" and found (that is, ordinary) movement as acceptable, even valued, materials, stimulated my curiosity about life at large. My life in 1964 was still organized around pastimes, studies, maintenance, and art events. I hardly noticed what was going on around me and nothing of what was going on inside me. I was continually astonished by incidents like those involving the art dealer; they seemed to me to come out of the blue, to be inexplicable, like forces of nature. A shift in emphasis from art to life finally seemed necessitated by problems incurred as a result of ignoring life. Dwelling on my life at that time meant an emotional immersion in it, as if it were a soap opera, but I was too immersed in it to know what it was. First during that year I was immersed in being enchanted by my new friend. Next I was immersed in my fears of abandonment and the abysmal feelings associated with rejection. As soon as the attentions of my friend's admirer became known, I assumed that all was lost. After that, all I had left to do was to react, and by thus reacting I assume I had already rejected the relationship. Having capitulated my identity, such as it was, how would I ever get it back? The fear of abandonment was rooted in this problem. If I were abandoned, where would I (my identity) be then? I had given myself over completely to this obviously superior being—a state of affairs I found unacceptable. Emotionally here, I was the girl. By contrast, my friend was aloof and contained. I never saw her own inner turmoil. She was no doubt the androgynous link between me and the man. For me the ideal object was a hidden man in a woman's form. The man hidden in me was much too deeply buried to be articulate; the man in me really was a depth charge, timed to explode whenever the appearances of my life crumbled. That time was now not far off. The signs of my dilemma were manifest all around me. The skirmishes between me and the art dealer, if they could be called that, were like the popping, hissing, bursting noises that precede massive eruptions. One classic scene between me and my friend, precipitated by my coming home to find a note she had written saying she was out with our knight the painter—acting out betrayal and abandonment and reconciliation by means of alcohol (I bought a pint of whiskey instantly) and tale-bearing (I told Charlotte everything) and unfaithfulness of my own (I found a strange man to fuck) and threats of violence (I hurled an ironing board through the atmosphere) and departure (I slammed out of the apartment in the small hours) and yielding (over bacon and eggs at a greasy spoon on Sixth Avenue at five a.m., after my friend followed me) —was proof positive of (impending) disaster. More interesting signs around me were the mysterious forms of personal imprint in art, the ones I would never have detected or deciphered or connected with my life, even when I wrote about them.

A dance that sculptor Robert Morris presented in March '65 sublimely expressed the function of my lover as medium between me and the male principle. Evidently Morris had perceived her masculine aspect where I had not. The stand-in for me was Rainer, who lived with Morris at that time. The dance was a trio in which Morris exalted himself and Rainer as a couple in paradise before the fall. The central image consisted of the two of them, naked and locked in an embrace, walking ever so slowly, accompanied by a lush aria from Verdi's *Simon Boccanegra*, on a twenty-foot length of wooden track running from center stage into the wings. The image was completed by my friend dressed as a man (hat, suit, tie) walking just upstage of them, holding a ball of twine stretched in a taut line over her shoulder into the wing behind them, unwinding as she walked. In other sections of the dance my friend performed "masculine functions"—moving props around or holding one end of a prop (a long pole) while Morris held the other end and ran round in circles, like the pointer on a compass. The woman in the dance (Rainer) had the passive part, Morris obviously the active, and my friend something in between.

The part I played was excited spectator, then approving

critic. In May I wrote a rave review of the dance, further
linking my friend with Morris by including in my piece a
review of a dance she had presented earlier, in January, featuring football as the ostensible subject. There was no football action per se, there were just a series of solo images
suggested by an edited, taped broadcast of a championship
game. So far as I knew, my friend was not particularly interested in football, nor could her presentation of herself ever
have been called butch or masculine. Yet there was nothing
especially feminine about her performance either, if feminine
means soft, romantic, sentimental, coy, decorative, submissive, or sexy. Her beauty had a mysterious, remote, hypnotic,
even catatonic quality; she was an astral sort of being, a limpid
character set in brittle diamond, a fairy-tale ice queen. Her
style was plain and cool and matter-of-fact. The veneer of
acceptability was vital to my sense of well-being. I felt I
could hide behind it; I had no such operable synthesis of
sexual properties. Though I now wore my lay-about preppy
clothes again, and imitated my friend in other ways, my own
lack of sexual definition was not transcendent like hers. It
was instead something nonnegotiable, rather like a counter-
feit bill with a figure on either side whose sexual disguises
were indecipherable.

Two years earlier, another male artist, sensitive to the
ambiguities of sex around him, had seized an image of me
and tried to cast it in some way similar perhaps to the use
Robert Morris made of my friend in his romantic trio. The
moment came soon after the assassination of JFK. The day
of the funeral I was in New Jersey at Billy Kluver's house
with Andy Warhol shooting one of his "home movies." I ran
around in circles in the mud wearing a red blazer and beret
and cutoff jeans and black boots and hauling a rifle. Later
that night in New York, at a party, Larry Rivers saw me in
this outfit and asked me to pose in it as a Moon Woman, a
life-sized portrait next to one of an astronaut as Moon Man.

The image wasn't characteristic of my appearance at the time, but Rivers must have seen something prophetic in it; I saw nothing at all. Anyway, I was mainly in ladies' drag then. And later on, in '64–'65, as mentioned, I regressed to a sexually undifferentiated look. Alas, I was a kind of aging *garçon manqué*. Hiding behind a "proper" girl was not the same as the respectable façade of a marriage, and I made one vain attempt of my own that season to legitimize my image through a male. The occasion was a gala festival of the Arts in Buffalo in February. The male was Robert Morris himself, always available to perform in pieces by others, or at least pieces by women. Morris was the only artist of stature in the Judson group other than Rauschenberg, and while he was not as big as Rauschenberg, his star as a sculptor was rising, and he was an impressive masculine sort of male— strong, cool, confident, and taciturn. At this festival in Buffalo I presented my favorite choreographers, including Morris, and under separate billing I did one of my "lecture events," which combined action tableaux with readings from passages about art and quotes from other sources. In this instance I asked Morris to build a simple two-by-four structure with a cross beam from which at some point I could hang. I wanted it to be so unsteady that it would collapse and crash around me as soon as I hung all my weight on it, and so while I talked at a mike he assembled this "bad" structure, and at the end I walked over and hung on it and tumbled down in a clatter of broken wood. From a symbolic point of view this was perhaps interesting, but as an event it left something to be desired, and I felt terminally mortified in the aftermath. Symbolically speaking, the whole festival was wrapped up for me by *Life* magazine. Composers, choreographers, and artists had participated in the festival. The layout of photographs in *Life* looked like a conspiracy to end my relationship. The lead page of the spread featured a full-color photo of my friend in a stunning pose from the dance she presented there, and alongside it a photo of one of my competitor's brilliant color-field paintings, incidentally called "Orange Crush," and included in the photo as silhouettes against the painting, *two nuns*. Even then the sorcery of this kind of collaging was not entirely wasted on me. The layout upset me for days. But while I knew a man in the art department of *Life* who could have been responsible for it, I assumed that it had happened for impersonal artistic reasons; it may have too, but I know now as I didn't then that the "artistic" manipulation of images is always informed by a wish.

The wish in this case, if not personally malicious, was nothing more than a desire to see tradition served by the proper meeting of some knight and his chosen princess. The male artist and female dancer were an ideal couple in our world. I wanted this myself of course, though at suicidal cost. What I wanted in effect was to see the two projected parts of myself, the knight and his princess, the artist and his dancer, ride off into the sunset together to make me whole—that is, dead—in lieu of the fact that I was not a proper half. I was condemned as a girl, and I would never succeed as a boy in a world I had to share with "real boys." The world was no longer the place where I had once practiced being a boy away from the corruption of other boys who would treat me like a girl, and where my identity as a girl among other girls was never in question. Nor was it the place, later on, where I could successfully pretend to be the kind of girl a boy in my family—father, brother, et al, had I had one—would have made me, by getting married. I had learned that a boy would try to turn me into a "real girl." And now I knew that a "real girl" would be surprised to learn that I was an incomplete version of herself, not to mention a failed boy. I desperately needed a new mentor, but not in the realm of the living. The time was approaching when at last my "dead father" would put in an appearance. In the meantime, as that winter thawed in '65, and in June I moved with my friend to a big loft, a summery reprieve was at hand.

The area I or we had chosen to move to was beautiful and cheap because it had been condemned by the city. The street was Liberty Street, where the World Trade Center now stands, and my friend was struck by the fact that the building address was the same as her parents' number uptown. Her suitor was out west for the summer; my children were in the country in Connecticut, once again with their grandmother. The days were halcyon and light blue—that's the way I remember them. On condemned property I imagined I was safe forever. My friend made her studio at one end of the loft, I had my desk and books at the other end, and the bed was in the middle. I had a new male friend who lived in a loft above us with his wife—they were the only other occupants of the building. I was living with an exotic, well-connected American girl, my male friend was an Irish Catholic Jew from Dublin who came to New York via Toronto, his wife was a Japanese woman born and raised in Canada. The book I was reading that excited me that summer was Norman O. Brown's *Life Against Death*. The most important thing I did personally was to give up smoking in June. The worst thing that happened was a fire in our loft caused by a urethane combustion. The strangest was an incident in the country involving my mother in late July.

Every Sunday as usual during the summer I drove up to see the children. On this particular Sunday in July I walked into my mother's summer cottage to find the living room turned into a gallery of portraits of myself aged several months through fifteen years, set out on all the tabletops. I was quite unprepared for such an exhibition, nor could I imagine what might have prompted it. My mother had ransacked one of her old trunks to surprise me. The children were dancing around and jumping up and down excitedly. I was embarrassed and confused. My mother's instinct for the inappropriate, the impulse by which she subverted her overextended manners, here seemed fully realized. Even when she told me why she had done it, I was no less dismayed; nonetheless I accepted

the spirit of her gesture in good faith. It was a curious moment indeed. Apparently my mother had made friends with
my old friend Marilyn from Washington Heights, the flaw-
less mother with twin girls, who with her husband owned the
side of a mountain not far from my mother's cottage. I had
often visited Marilyn there with my kids so they could all
play together and I could enjoy my friend's hospitality, and
as my mother knew nobody in the country with small children, I had encouraged her to know my friend. My mother
could appreciate a woman like Marilyn, who was practically
my age and who was so ideal, and Marilyn in turn could
appreciate my mother for being such a good grandmother.
My mother's habit of confiding her misgivings about me to
her friends was not entirely inhibited by these unusual circumstances; in fact she managed to convey both her fears for
me in the world and her personal resentment of how I treated
her. Most recently I had failed to appreciate her strenuous
efforts in caring for my children during the summer, and
since Marilyn was a proper mother she could understand my
mother's feelings. Had I known how my mother felt I might
have told her I thought she *wanted* the children. She did, of
course, but she also wanted a sign of recognition, and that
I was unable to give her because I took her for granted. As for
her fears for me in the world, on this score Marilyn was the
first person my mother ever knew who was in a position to
verify my career. Thus she told my mother that I was a
successful critic in New York. Immediate proof of this was
available, she told her, in an anthology just published called
The New American Arts, to which I had contributed the
essay about dance. This endorsement was so startling, so
unprecedented, so contrary to all my mother's ideas about
me, and so impossible to ignore, coming as it did from such
an admirable person as Marilyn, that my mother went over-
board to redress her sins of omission. She dove down to the
bottom of our past to recover the icons of our lost innocence

together. The exhibition of baby photos was like a wake: had I died, she might have set them out the same way. It looked as if something very big had taken place, when in fact all that had happened was that my mother had found out I had a career in New York. If she had wanted to shock me in turn, she had succeeded. "I knew her when . . ." smacks of great deeds and amazing exploits, but I had done nothing really, and I had every intention of continuing to confirm my mother's fears for me. I was horrified by any intimations of success. A photo of myself appeared on the back of the anthology among the six contributors; my mother ordered the book and enthusiastically had me sign her copy. In New York one Sunday I appeared in the Sunday *Times* dance column in a piece featuring dance critics of the so-called post-modern dance. That August I gave up dance criticism.

One way to end a career is to become hopelessly inflated about it. A fear of success may be well served by delusions of achievement. I was the product after all of an "ordinary middle-class family" in which no one had ever become public or prominent. I had gone far enough. As in a dream, perhaps, I collected these symbols of a success that I really meant to abort. I was still learning to be a critic. I had much to learn if I was to hit my stride or gain a mature perspective; instead, I was going to abandon my ambition in midstream. In August I experienced a massive regression. The baby pictures had spelled out my immediate future: my only certain identity was that as my mother's daughter. If my mother wanted me, as she so strikingly demonstrated, surely I could give up the world, which had proved so difficult, and return to our original circumstances. I had already done that in a sense by relinquishing my identity to my girl friend—I had become much more interested in her work than in mine. Having been an unsuccessful boy, I intended to retreat behind a successful girl, the girl not even my mother was able to be. But a successful girl would never find happiness with another girl; she had to go off with a successful boy. This would leave me free to go off altogether. That summer of 1965 I was, unbeknownst to myself, preparing to leave the world. The days that were halcyon and light blue got lighter and lighter. If I left first, as it were, I could provide the excuse for my friend to leave. I needed a boy too. And the boy one finds upon leaving the world is usually God the Father, the great unknown one. Having come into the world as a *fille de père inconnu*, it was fitting that I meet him at last. The next part of my life was to be an amazing interlude, a two-year period in which I made a double hairpin turn in slow motion around myself in preparation for reentering the world, and subsequently going abroad to discover my actual father and/or his remains. Only a father's daughter, or son, could function in a world governed by fathers; eventually that came clear to me. The essence of this story is how I learned to make it my own.